SLEEPING IN DIXIE'S

FEATHER BED

GROWING UP WHITE
IN THE SEGREGATED SOUTH

LOU ELLEN WATTS

SLEEPING IN DIXIE'S FEATHER BED

ISBN: 978-0-9963949-7-0

10 9 8 7 6 5 4 3 2 1

The picture of Martin Luther King on the cover is credited to History. com. Historical information has been gleaned from various shared information sites on the Internet. Georgetown history is recorded in the illustrated book *Georgetown and the Waccamaw Neck in Vintage Postcards* by Susan Hoffer McMillan and *A Guide to the City of Georgetown Historic District,* 1995 edition, published by the Georgetown County Historical Society. Photos are from the author's personal collections unless otherwise noted.

Printed in the United States of America

Hawthorne Publishing
15601 Oak Road
Carmel In 46033
317-867-5183 Hawthornepub.com

This book is for Ervin, the most wonderful husband and the light of my life.

I want to express my thanks to Hawthorne Publishing, my publisher, which has released over 300 books of regional history for thirty years in Indiana and accepted my book into the line although it is not within their usual historical publishing limits. Art Baxter, president, served as this book's designer, and Nancy Baxter was its awesome editor. They helped me put all these memories on paper.

Lou Ellen Watts

PREFACE

My three-year-old son and I were visiting my parents in a little town in northern Louisiana where I had spent my high school days. I was in a graduating class of 150 students—all white. In my high school eyes, the entire town was white. Of course, there were blacks in the town, but my world was all white...white churches, white restaurants, white schools, white parks, white movie houses, white buses, white everything. My husband and I had been gone from the South for many years and were living in Arizona. I wondered if things had changed much since I left.

My mother needed some things from the grocery store, so I loaded Billy, our son, into the car. She told me the new store, Piggly Wiggly, had opened and I should go there. After some turns and stoplights I located the store. I pulled into a parking space near the entrance. As Billy and I began walking to the door he excitedly shouted, "Look Mama, look! There's a clown!" "Where, Billy?" I asked, thinking that a clown might be entertaining children in the store. He pointed and said, "Over there by the door."

Next to the side door of the grocery store was an ordinary black man dressed in ordinary clothes. "Be quiet, Billy," I said. "That's not a clown. It's a black man. I'll explain later." I was, of course, concerned the man would be insulted if he heard Billy calling him a clown.

Later that night, I realized our son had never been aware of a person's color. I tried to think if he had even seen a black person. We had lived in the southwest for many years and had many Hispanic friends whose skin was not as light as ours but still not as dark as many African Americans. There were only a few people with dark skin in our lives.

If Billy had been brought up in this southern part of the United States, he would have been aware of different skin tones. He would have immediately distinguished the difference between a clown and an African American. Unaware of color—that was how my husband and I wished to bring up our son.

How did I escape the bondage of thinking in two-tone mentality? What would have become of my own view if I had not wandered away from this locality and had stayed there, sleeping blissfully away in Dixie's soft, views-conditioned feather bed? If I had stayed, would I have been forced to put on blinders and only see what was in front of me, or would I have punched holes in these obstructions to peek out to see what was right before my face?

I had lived, grown up really, in the South for twenty-two years and considered it my home. It was only when I escaped that I came to realize the plight of African Americans still striving to be recognized as people. Rising up from the distorted views in Dixie to face the real world had not been easy, but I had done it. This is that story.

GEORGETOWN

SOUTH CAROLINA 1940-1952

THE CLEANING GIRL

I was born in Georgetown, South Carolina, in 1940, the midst of the Depression: people in the South and all over the United States were struggling to survive. Both whites and blacks lived from day to day, and if they were without jobs, they had no fallback and no assistance program. I was born to a middle-class family; around us were many whose lot was worse. Most of the colored people in the South were sharecroppers, tenant farmers, or farm laborers, barely subsisting from year to year. In 1936, South Carolina was one of six states without old-age pensions, one of fourteen without assistance for the blind, and one of two with no aid for dependent children. In 1937, some of these groups were included, but the early Social Security program in South Carolina overlooked a large number of people. Farm and domestic workers were not included; therefore, most colored people were not eligible.

My parents, Dollie and Bernie Overhultz, and my three-year-old sister Margaret had moved from Arkansas to Georgetown, South Carolina, when a new mill of the International Paper Company had opened in 1936. There were so many people coming in to work that there was a shortage of houses, and people rented out rooms in their homes. Small apartments opened up over grocery stores, and my parents found a small upstairs apartment near downtown and moved into it with my sister. I was born four years later, but my mother and father had differences, so my father took me to live in an apartment in a different part of town, leaving my sister with my mother. She may have suffered from what we call today postpartum depression. Maybe she just didn't want to raise another child.

I never knew about my parents' separation until I went with my father to get my marriage license in 1963. I presented my birth certificate to the marriage license official, and she pointed out that my name was printed, "NO NAME OVERHULTZ." It was then that my father told me about the separation, but he didn't give any explanation about the reconciliation that had obviously occurred by the time I could notice life in our home.

Perhaps Mother might have remembered how hard it was growing up with twelve siblings whose father was a poor sharecropper in rural Arkansas, and felt conflicted about children. She had told me that when she was young, all of the older boys and girls would pull burlap sacks out into the fields in the summer and pick the white cotton bolls off the dried stalks. The Arkansas sun had beaten down on them; her back hurt when she came home after sundown.

When school was in session, the children would pile into the farm wagon and hitch the old horse up and drive to the one-room school down the road. In the warm weather they went barefoot, but they always carried their lunch of a biscuit and a piece of cheese in their tin pails. All thirteen children were left in a desperate situation when their mother died of cancer at the age of 44. I asked Mother to tell me about my grandmother. "She was beautiful and so sweet," she said. Then she started talking about how they took care of her when she had cancer. "Every once in a while, my father would go into the bedroom and give her a shot for the pain. Once they brought in an Indian who did some kind of healing ceremony, but it never got better. The night she died, I ran off in the woods to a neighbor's house. I was eighteen and stayed there for a few years taking care of their house and baby until I got a job at the paper mill in Arkadelphia. That's where I met your father."

Georgetown was growing, and a new section of town in the country was being developed when my parents looked for a spot for their family. My father had a house built on a gravel road where only a few houses dotted the landscape between the trees and tall weeds. This road came to an end when it reached the Yawkey Wildlife Reserve, where the only access to the island was by a pull ferry. The house with white asbestos shingles had two bedrooms, one bath, a living room, and a kitchen. A back porch was added later and also a pull-down ladder for access to the attic. Whenever my parents weren't looking, I would swing on the gate of the little picket fence that enclosed the area next to the front kitchen door. Electricity didn't extend much further down the road from our house, so very few white people lived past us, and only a few colored people lived in shacks down in the swampy area. Occasionally, a single car or truck would pass down the road, stirring up dust and slinging rocks in our yard. Each morning the big yellow school bus lumbered down the road and picked up white children, and each afternoon the same bus stopped to let the same children off.

Mother did all the housework with no hired help except for an occasional poor colored person who dropped by looking for work. It was very common in those days for people to stop at houses for various reasons: encyclopedia salesmen came to the door, and occasionally photographers would try to convince the woman of the house to have her children's pictures taken. I remember watching with fascination as a vacuum cleaner salesman demonstrated the latest machine. Trucks filled with produce would pull off into the driveways to display their fresh vegetables. Most people in the country, though, grew their own vegetables, so the vendors didn't make much money selling to them.

One summer morning in about 1943 a truck filled with colored people stopped in front of our house. There were perhaps six men seated in the back, with two in the cab of the truck next to the driver. The cab door opened, and a small colored girl wearing a short, faded flour-sack dress got out, then slowly walked to the house while the truck waited. When she got to the front door, she turned and waved at the driver. The truck, on its way to drop off colored laborers at a job, crunched into gear and went on down the road.

Since there was no air conditioning in those days, the doors and windows of our house were left open during the summer to let the cool breeze in. Screens were attached to all of the windows to keep the bugs out, but were always kept latched. My mother must have heard the little girl knock and gone to the front door. I was just a little girl, following her around. Odd that I can remember the details of this when I was only three and half or so, but I do. She stopped at the screen door and stared at the old truck going down the road, then began talking with the colored girl. She soon held the screen open and let her in. The girl and I stared at each other while my mother went out to the kitchen and brought back rags and furniture polish. She said something to the girl then took me by the hand and led me out of the room to the kitchen. I stared; who was this? A child older than I but looking different from me.

The kitchen with its eating area was the hub of our house. Here my mother spent a lot of time cooking, sewing, and washing clothes. In the winter my parents closed off the rest of the house and heated the kitchen area with the gas stove and a small porcelain heater. They took the tall brown Philco radio in there and listened to the news and music. In the early spring and early fall, the radio was carried back into the front room again, and there at night my father sat in his big brown chair reading and listening to baseball games.

I had experienced little association with colored folk. My introduction, both then and later, was partially conditioned by radio programs, which presented Negros in the way the culture viewed them. One of the most popular radio shows in those days was *Amos 'n' Andy*, where white actors spoke the lines of colored people. What some of these shows did was present these people as stereotypical dummies who talked in exaggerated dialect and made stupid decisions—as bumbling idiots. So my small self had little information on another race, and what I did have was false. And now, here was a real live colored person in my house.

After lunch I sneaked away from my mother and came back to the front room to see this stranger. Since it was a hot summer day, I had on only little white cotton underpants that hung loosely on my bottom. My three-year-old feet slid over the cool oak floors and stopped next to my favorite rocking chair, which had arms that looked like swans. The girl was on her knees polishing the rungs of the rocker and looked up as I came nearer. Her hair wasn't white, and it was dressed in cornrows the way the colored girls did when they were young. Her skin was shiny and she had a fresh soap smell, so I ventured a little closer and sat down next to her. She looked up at me and smiled but continued her work. Something in this smile made me want to know her so I leaned over even closer and watched as she hummed a little melody and continued polishing the chair.

Later in the afternoon, the same truck filled with the colored workers stopped in front of the house. I watched my mother as she went to the colored girl and gave her a coin. The little stranger pushed the screen door open and skipped to the truck, which left in a cloud of dust.

It didn't matter that her skin was a different color than mine. In fact, I probably didn't notice that hers was dark and mine was light. She was just a girl in a short, faded flour-sack cotton dress who stopped her work polishing the furniture for a moment to give me a smile.

By the early forties, the Depression seemed to be over, but most colored families still struggled to make ends meet in our mill community. The income of rural colored people was about half that of rural whites. The war had brought increased military spending, which opened many opportunities for the white working class, but preferences for hiring whites over colored dominated. One of the slogans that referred to the colored workers was, "Last Hired, First Fired."

Blacks and whites had to face the war. World War II brought many shortages for our entire community and the nation. In Georgetown, as elsewhere, the government issued coupons, ration stamps. Adults were given small booklets with a certain number of stamps according to how many people there were in the family. My parents would go to the post office in Georgetown each month to get ration stamps for our family. Sugar was first rationed, but later cheese, butter, canned milk, cooking oil, metals, meat, some canned goods, and almost everything valuable to the war effort was included in the list. Families couldn't buy certain items at the grocery store unless they gave the grocer the correct ration stamp from their booklets. Gasoline was in a short supply, as were tires for cars. Even driving for sightseeing was banned, and a speed limit of 35 miles an hour was enforced to save on gasoline in many places.

People were encouraged to help the war effort. We would peel the foil off any candy or gum wrappers and roll it into balls; when a ball got big enough, we would take it to the collection department. We saved metal toothpaste tubes and tin cans and were encouraged to save hairpins, then take them back to the beauty salon at our next visit. Cooking oil was used over and over until it was no longer fresh. It was then taken to the local butcher, where after collection, it was shipped to processing centers for use in making items like glycerin.

There was no television in those days, so in our living room we listened to news on the radio or read the limited newspapers. Headlines came in about the movement of the Nazis into Poland and France and the devastating bombings of Britain. My father was not drafted into the service because of foot problems, but he brought home news from the paper mill where he worked and from the Aircraft Warning Service for which he volunteered. On certain days and nights he would be given field glasses and was assigned locations to scan the horizon for incoming enemy planes. U-boats had been spotted in the bays off the ocean in our area, so these threats were real.

Georgetown was near the military bases at Myrtle Beach and Charleston and, the government said, lights from the mill could provide enemy planes methods to calculate distances from the paper mill to these bases. Even though we lived out in the country, we could still hear multiple short siren blasts from the mill alerting the town to upcoming danger or possible war-connected disasters. When the employees heard the blast signal, they would rush to the mill and take assigned jobs, while the families at home went inside and waited for the siren to give the long all-clear signal. If the siren blasts were given at night, the paper mill turned its lights out and would go on limited production. When we heard the alert signal, Father would leave in the car and my mother would turn off the lights, pull the dark green blackout window shades down, and wait in the dark for the long all clear siren blast from the mill.

During one of these blackouts, my father left for the mill and my mother, aunt, sister, and I sat on the bed in my parents' room with the lights out and the blackout shades pulled down. My aunt pulled back one of the shades and looked out to see if there were any enemy planes in the sky, then looked toward downtown to see if any airplanes had dropped bombs on the paper mill or on the harbor. My sister yelled at her to keep the shade closed so no light would escape and alert the enemy.

Colored people beyond our neighborhood must have done the same thing. Both races sent soldiers to Europe and the Pacific theaters of war. Families of white men as well as colored men were wrapped up in thoughts of their sons and brothers far from home. We experienced the war, but just as we did everything else in those times, we must have experienced the situation around us differently.

THE YARD MAN

It was about 1948 and World War II was over. My parents could throw away, or put in a drawer, ration stamps, and meat and gasoline became available again. The average salary in America was $3,600, postage stamps were three cents, and cars averaged $1,550. New items like Reynolds Wrap, Ajax cleanser, and Prell shampoo showed up at our grocery store. The year before, Bazooka bubble gum made its way onto the market. My older sister and I would each get a piece, chew it all day long, then put it in the freezer so it would stay clean. We'd chew it again the next day. Five cents was a lot of money for this delicious, interesting stuff. I would put my gum on one side of the overhead freezer, and she would put hers on the other side. We tried to make sure we chewed the correct piece.

Down the road from our house were those colored-people shacks that had always hovered there, all through the war, but we weren't concerned about them. We were more interested in exploring our little neighborhood and discovering what was new to us. Our property was set on an acre of land lined in the front by a dusty two-lane road and in the back by tall trees. A weedy lot with scattered pine trees and marshy ponds was on one side, with our driveway running parallel to the neighbor's house. No one had a large green yard out there in the country, but everyone tried to keep the weeds under control. My sister and I had a large swing in the backyard, but there were so many sand burrs around it that we never ventured there without shoes.

On spring days my friends and I would wander the countryside, picking wild violets, lilies, and pitcher plants. We tied them up into little bouquets with pine needles and took them to our mothers. Sometimes we would pull petals off the wildflowers, place them on the bare green stems, and pretend our creations were little people dressed for a royal ball. In the summer we put on tall boots to keep the snakes, chiggers, and stickers off and would go pick wild blackberries that we knew our mothers would make into blackberry pies. What were those colored children down among those trees and bogs doing? We didn't know and didn't care. Probably they had some of the same activities.

The long summer days were spent outside with the neighbor children: Johnny, who was my elementary school boyfriend; Eddy, his younger brother; and Kathleen, my best girlfriend. We hid in the pine trees and pretended we were fairies or wild animals who roamed in secret. The smelly pine sap stuck on our fingers as we pulled it off the bark and chewed it like chewing gum. It tasted nasty, but we chewed it anyway.

Farther down the road was another clump of trees that surrounded a small house. I always wondered who lived there, since I never saw anyone going in or coming out of the house. One summer day, we decided to explore that clump of trees and boldly walked down the road, past the strange house, and right to the trees. I was very nervous about going onto another person's property, and I asked Johnny who lived there. He told me it was an old woman whose husband had died in the war. This answer didn't make me feel any better, but I followed him anyway.

Underneath the trees was a child's fantasy land...old bottles, rusty cans, discarded shoes, and broken furniture. All of a sudden I spotted a strange object. It was a rusty green cylinder about four feet long. I shouted to Johnny, "Get over here quick! Look at what I found!"

All of them ran over and stood frozen. Finally, Johnny said, "It's a bomb." He and his brother were always playing war and pretending they were throwing grenades and bombs at imaginary enemies, so I figured he knew what a bomb looked like. Also, it looked like one of those bombs falling from planes that we had seen in newsreels at the movies.

We thought this was a real "find" and knew we had to take it home. Grabbing sticks, we frantically began digging the bomb out of the encasing dirt. Finally, we pulled it up and started down the road to Johnny's house. Johnny held up the front of the bomb, Eddie was on the back end, and Kathleen and I held on to the sides. It was heavy, but we were determined to take our "find" to show our parents. When we got to Johnny's house, we put the bomb on the back porch steps and called for his father. "Look what we found!" we proudly said. I didn't know why his father had a panicked look on his face when he saw this bomb. He told us to lug it out into one of the fields and to never go near it again. Sometime later he had someone from the military base in Charleston go out and blow the bomb up. The official told him that occasionally a bomb would accidentally fall off a plane and land in a field unnoticed, and there was no way he could trace the origin of that particular bomb. Sometimes it still haunts my thoughts of the past.

Whenever we found a dead bird, we would put it in a matchbox or wrap it in toilet paper and carry it to the tall trees in back of our property for a funeral. We would put the dead bird in a hole that someone had dug earlier and gather around in a circle for a ceremony. Someone sang a hymn, followed by a prayer. Wild berries grew in abundance, and we would mash the wine-colored berries up and stir them in water for pretend wine to use for the wake or reception. We would never drink this wine because we were told that these berries could be poisonous. Other times we would grind up bark from the wild sassafras bushes to use for tea. If we were lucky, someone would have raided his or her mother's cabinet and brought a cookie for each of us. What a tight little group we were, having these backyard funerals! We never thought about which church each of us went to. Our only thought was to ask God to accept these poor birds into bird heaven.

Since my father hadn't been in the army and didn't need to readjust to normal life after returning, like many men around us, my parents continued to be settled in their comfortable routine. The South Carolina soil in this part of the state seemed to be just sand, and as my mother would say, "This dirt is not good for growing much of anything." In spite of that, my mother grew a garden with beans, carrots, tomatoes, and peas. My parents raised chickens and at one time owned a cow named Betsy. Twice a day, my mother milked her but got mad because the cow kept getting loose and would wander off into the woods. They sold Betsy after a few months.

My father loved to hunt and would get his rifle and venture off into the woods in search of ducks and rabbits. Frog legs were considered a culinary delicacy in the area, so in the summer he would go out into the marsh ponds out back and catch frogs. When he brought them home, he would skin the legs and give them to my mother, who would fry them in Crisco. Sometimes when she dropped them into the hot oil they would jerk and wiggle like they were still alive. My sister wouldn't eat any, but I thought they tasted just like chicken.

We were just a typical middle-class country family in the late forties and early fifties. My mother cooked, cleaned, and sewed while my father worked various shifts at the paper mill. My sister and I helped with the chores and tended our very own marigold gardens. I was always competing with her on everything, so I was ecstatic that my marigolds seemed to be taller than hers.

One of my chores was collecting the chicken eggs. I would take the egg bucket, unlatch the gate, and sneak into the enclosure, making sure the chickens didn't get out. In the summer I never wore shoes unless I was going to church or running through the woods, so I didn't have a problem with the chicken poop ruining my shoes. Before I took the eggs to the house, I would sit on a stump and use a stick to pick the green chicken poop out from between my toes. If I had to go inside the house, my mother would make me wash my feet at the outside faucet before I went in. I was hardly ever inside the house during the summer days, so she didn't really have to worry about my tracking chicken poop into the house.

During those days, most people around us didn't have luxuries: washing machines and gas lawnmowers were for others or the future. So at times the workload was overwhelming for both women and men. One day my father dropped a colored man off at our house. It was a warm sunny day when I first saw him in the backyard holding a rake and hoe. He had on black pants and a khaki shirt with patched pockets. Even though it was late spring, the man sported a faded beige felt hat that was covered with layers of dust. I looked at him and supposed he was there to work in our yard. There wasn't much grass to mow, so I hoped he would cut down the sand burrs next to the swings and not disturb my marigold plants.

Even though my father had hired him to do yard work, as soon as he got there that morning, my mother appropriated him. She led him to the chicken yard, where on her instructions, he grabbed one of the chickens. He took it to a stump, put the chicken's neck on it, and chopped its head off. This was probably going to be our dinner. Usually my mother would wring the chicken's neck first, then chop its head off. When the poor chicken stopped flopping around on the ground, my mother soaked it in boiling water to loosen the feathers so she could pluck them off. I would cry when I watched the poor chickens meet their deaths and flop around.

Sometimes she would have my sister pluck the feathers off, but thankfully I was too young. No doubt it wasn't her favorite job, so she was glad to see the colored helper that day. And it was a different way, I thought, of dispatching a chicken, with a hatchet.

My mother always cooked a large noonday meal for what was then called dinner. She usually started preparing the meal about 11 o'clock so we could eat precisely at noon when my father came home. Meat had been rationed just before this period, so we had learned to eat a lot of chicken, and we always had rice, which had once been the main crop of our area, with each meal. Sometimes leftover rice was stirred into scrambled eggs and served with grits and bacon for breakfast. I also remember Mother spooning out some leftover rice in a cup, covering it with canned milk and a little sugar, and giving it to us for breakfast. We ate a lot of cornbread, fruit cobblers, and ham, along with the vegetables from the garden. My mother would boil up a batch of turnip greens and stir a little bacon fat into it, but no one in our family would eat the greens except Mother, unless it was New Year's Day. The custom in the South was to eat black-eyed peas with a helping of greens on New Year's Day for good luck. I ate the peas and always tried to swallow one slimy string of greens.

But now this new person, this hired man, was here at the house. I watched him for a while. At noon a car drove up, and we knew it was my father, come home to eat. The colored man sat in the backyard under our dogwood tree waiting for his food. It was custom for the owners of the house to give the workers food as well as pay. My mother scooped a helping of chicken and rice on a piece of newspaper and took it to the colored man. He didn't have a plate or even a spoon but only a piece of newspaper with food on it.

After our family finished its meal, my mother told me to go ask the man if he wanted some more to eat. Hesitantly, I went to the screen door and watched him as he licked the newspaper to get the last piece of food off. Without asking, I could see that he still looked hungry. "He wants some more," I called out. My mother dished out some more rice with a few chicken pieces onto another piece of newspaper. I held the meal out to him and watched as he scooped the rice up with his black fingers then lowered his eyes and said, "Thank you." I frowned. Why couldn't he have a plate and spoon to eat with like I did? Questions like this would be taking me on a long road down the pike.

During those segregated days, colored people where I lived were not supposed to touch a white person's hand or to ever have eye contact with them. Some states even had laws that prohibited colored people from using the same plates and utensils as white people. Perhaps my mother didn't want the colored man to eat off her dishes or use one of her spoons. Did she think the utensils would become contaminated? Did she worry the plate could have been broken? Would she have provided a plate and spoon if this had been a white person doing the yard work? I'll never know because it wasn't discussed.

That night I snuggled under my bed cover and thought about that man eating off a piece of newspaper. I thought to myself, "That's the way we feed our dog and cat! My family's dinner plates aren't fancy and our spoons aren't silver, but they're better than eating off newspaper like that poor colored man did."

The last thing I remember before closing my eyes that night was hoping he had a good meal when he got home to his own house and was able to eat it on a plate with a spoon.

DAYS AT THE OCEAN

To this day, even though I live far from the ocean, I can hear it echoing in my mind from my earliest childhood times in South Carolina. This must be how the planters' children of ante-bellum times felt, and they too must have recalled it mournfully in different days after the Civil War, when they had fallen on hard times, remembering the dunes, the grasses and screaming seagulls not far from lovely homes. The rich children of my own days would probably hear the echoes of the ocean in South Carolina all their lives. The ocean knew no classes, no differences in the people who visited it.

Rich plantation owners had summer homes on these Carolina beaches. Pawleys Island was separated from the mainland by marshes. Malaria-carrying mosquitoes couldn't get over to the island. This became a refuge for the wealthy planters who dominated our country in former days. Even today families continued to stay on these islands during the summer, while many lived there year round. And our family enjoyed it too.

The summers spent in the 1940s and 1950s on Pawleys Island were the most exciting times a child could have. Trips there to visit friends, swim in the frothy water, collect seashells, and catch crabs with long blue claws are stored in my memory. There were sunny days on the beach when we got blistered and turned as brown as South Carolina sea grasses. And there were cloudy days when our lips turned blue while we shivered in the salt water, still begging our mothers to let us stay in for just a little longer.

Gales and storms on the Atlantic Ocean excited the senses: waves slapping on the beach, the pungent smell of the salt air seeping into our noses, the sand blown by the wind that jabbed our skin, the taste of the brine sweeping past our lips. When the sky turned from gray to black and the electricity failed, the grownups lit the kerosene lanterns in the cabins where we stayed and the children huddled together to listen to ghost stories about the gray lady or the lost lover who washed up on the beach and walked the dunes looking for his way home.

Sometimes we would stay with our friends at their beach house. It was a typical wooden house built up on stilts. Stairs that led to the main part of the house were built underneath the house on its concrete pad. Before we climbed the stairs we always had to rinse our feet with a chain pulled shower so the beach sand wouldn't track into the house.

Usually, other guests with young children and teenagers had been invited. The anticipation of getting into the water was almost unbearable, but my sister and I knew we had to be polite and talk to the grownups for a few minutes. Finally, they gave the signal and all of us bounded out to the frigid ocean.

Swimming and playing in the water always made us hungry, so we welcomed lunch, even though we had to wait an hour before we could go back in. While we waited that hour, we would go outside and play in the sand and "doodle" for doodle bugs. We would twirl a stick in the hole where these little insects hung out and say, "Doodle bug, doodle bug, come out your hole." Whenever a bug would come out, we'd pinch it and put it in a bottle. As soon as the novelty of that was worn off, we would go to the screen porch and swing in the hammock to see who could go the highest.

When the sun started going down, excitement built again as we collected driftwood to make a bonfire to roast wieners. The men stacked the wood and started the blaze. Each person grabbed a coat hanger that had been straightened in the shape of a spear and put a wiener on it. After the hot dogs were eaten and marshmallows were toasted, the teenagers climbed the dunes to escape the world of grownups. While the fire blazed the younger children leaned against their parents and listened to the steady lull of the ocean. At night the grownups would sleep in the main part of the house while the children and teenagers slept on the screen porch on cots or in hammocks.

These Pawleys Island hammocks were designed by a riverboat captain in 1889 so his crew could have a comfortable way to sleep. They were seen on almost every porch on the island. The ropes of the hammocks pressed marks on our faces as we were rocked to sleep by the wind. Sometimes before we fell asleep we could see fishermen with lanterns and gig poles wading in the knee deep water of the inlets. The light attracted flounder, and with great accuracy the men would spear these flat fish and drop them into burlap bags wrapped around their waists. The lanterns looked like small fairy lights floating across the black water.

The next morning while the adults packed the car, we would head to the ocean for one last swim. The departure time came and we started to the car. As we scuttled along, we were aware how the wind had blown sand into our hair and how it had seeped into our ears. We pulled at our swimsuits and brushed our arms and legs, but it was impossible to get all the sand off before we got into the car. The salt water that was drying on our skin became sticky and irritated our blistered, sunburned skin. While we struggled with all of these irritations we knew that this was the last time to say goodbye to our friends before we headed home.

The older I got the more I longed for the mystical times when I slept on an island and the wind rocked me to sleep in a Pawleys Island hammock.

Myrtle Beach was another destination of my childhood. During the 1940's an Air Force base was established there for training soldiers during WWII. Right after the war the beautiful beaches were filled with so many tourists that it was hard to find a place to swim. But we really came because of the amusement park and the pavilion. The amusement park opened in 1948 after a traveling carnival made its home permanent along the beach. It was built across from the pavilion that had been rebuilt many times since its origin in the early 1900's.

You could still see how the amusement park had been created from that carnival, whose owner had the Big Top's ropes and chains pounded into the ground to make it permanent. There were rides, booths with games, side shows, and food. We waited for the cotton candy machine to puff its pink sugary treat into the metal tub, then watched while the attendant reached in and wound it on a long stick. I remember clutching my cotton candy and climbing into one of the gondolas of the Ferris wheel with my father. We both grinned as we went round and round, but as soon as we got off I almost cried when I saw that the wind had dissolved my cotton candy into one hard sticky mess.

We didn't go to that amusement park at Myrtle Beach often as a family. I observed that high school students, older than I was, would drive there on Saturdays with their friends or go with their teenaged church groups. I remember my mother giving my sister some money for one of the trips and telling her that she had to be home before dark. I went to my mother and wanted to know why I couldn't go too. "It's for the older girls. Someday your turn will come." When my sister got home I had her tell me all about the rides and food.

Living so near the ocean and its bays and inlets created a perfect opportunity for us to get involved with water sports and activities. My father would often take his little paddle boat on weekends, launch it in one of the inlets and bring home fish for supper. My mother loved to fish, but she never had the time to take off from daily chores. However, she took charge whenever the parents decided to go catch crabs.

I jumped for joy when Mother unexpectedly announced that we were going crabbing the next day. My sister and I got up early in the morning and scrambled to get our beach things together. Mother made sandwiches and filled thermoses with water and lemonade. Daddy's job was to get the bait lines and buckets ready and store them in our car's trunk. I can still hear my mother asking my father, "Did you get enough crab bait from the store?" She was always worried that we might run out and not be able to get anymore where we went on to Pawley's Island.

Margaret and I loaded ourselves into the back of our two-door Ford sedan while our parents checked and rechecked the supplies. While we waited, the two of us talked about a previous trip with our mother and our Aunt Christine: Mother was driving and instinctively slowed down when my aunt yelled out, "Look! There's a wallet on the side of the road." She began to pull off to the side of the road when Aunt Christine said, "Don't stop. Colored people put wallets out in the road so the white people will stop. Then they could get us." From that day on I thought I'd better watch the side of the road for wallets and the colored people who were out to get us.

The folks finally slammed the trunk of the car shut, got in the front seat, and took off toward Pawleys Island. We didn't have a radio in the car so we had to entertain ourselves. My sister read and I stared out the window, pretending I was lost in the thick pine trees I saw by the side of the road and had to find my way out. The trip seemed to be taking forever when my mother pointed to a sign and said, "Slow down. The turnoff's at the next road."

There were no big grocery stores on the beach, but little fish stands run by crusty residents dotted the side roads that led to long wooden piers. In addition to fishing supplies, the stands had candy bars, sodas and the south's famous boiled or roasted peanuts. Margaret convinced Daddy to stop at one of the stands and buy each of us a bottle of coke and a bag of shelled, roasted peanuts. We carefully opened the coke bottle, poured the peanuts into it, and then slurped it down. I really liked the boiled peanuts better than the roasted ones but I always copied my big sister.

My father continued driving down the asphalt road then turned onto a narrow path covered with seagrass and trash. He drove slowly, waiting for my mother to spot a good crabbing spot. It was early in the day, but colored people were already lining the canals with their lines and buckets. The residents usually knew good places to crab but my mother said, "The colored people always take the best spots. We can stop and ask them if they're having any luck." They didn't ask anyone about a good spot but pulled over to a flat place. Daddy opened the trunk of the car and unloaded the lines, buckets and crab bait. We each grabbed some buckets and began walking through the gooey, gray pluff mud that smelled like rotten shrimp. The mud made a sucking sound as we made our way to a spot where water was pooling. It was only inches deep in some places but we knew we had to be careful since it could get deeper and hold on to you like quick sand.

Several colored men with their crab lines and buckets were watching for signs of crabs that might be gnawing the bait. When they saw us, they nodded, then gathered their equipment and struggled up to the side of the road. I didn't know why they left. As I think about this now, I wonder if they left because they weren't catching anything or because they were intimidated by the whites invading their spot. Maybe they were wary, a little afraid.

After a morning of crabbing in the inlets, we made our way to the ocean and had our lunch on a blanket my mother laid out under one of the cabanas. The tide was out so this made for a wonderful time to collect seashells. Margaret and I walked the beach picking favorite shells to take home when I spotted an unusual one and brushed the sand off. It was all black with ridges on it. "Margaret, look at this one," I said. She looked at it and said,

"It's a nigger toe. "Why is it called that?" Nonchalantly she answered, "I don't know. I guess that's what their toes look like." I pulled at her hand and shouted, "Let's go look for whitey toes. I bet they'll look like ours."

At the end of the day we started our drive back home. It had been another wonderful day but as I looked out the window, I wondered where all the colored people had gone. I asked, "Where do the colored people swim?" It was always my sister who answered my questions and said, "They aren't allowed to swim in our area. They have their own beach." In one word I questioned, "Why?"

There was silence and I didn't pursue the answer. I watched out the window and looked for the colored people's beaches. I wondered if their beaches were different from ours and if they would let me swim with them.

SATURDAY DOWNTOWN—JUST THE WAY IT WAS

Georgetown, South Carolina, is a historic southern town located between Charleston and Myrtle Beach on Winyah Bay off the Atlantic Ocean. During the Revolutionary War, it was occupied by the British from July 1780 to May 1781. Many of its buildings were burned by a loyalist privateer. George Washington stayed in one of its houses during his 1791 southern tour of the thirteen colonies. He sent a letter to the inhabitants of Georgetown on April 30, 1791, that said, "I received your congratulations on my arrival in South Carolina with real pleasure, and I confess my obligation to your affectionate regard with sincere gratitude...."

Once this area had over fifty plantations, which used slave labor to work the fields. Indigo was the main crop, followed by rice. After the Civil War, timber became the most profitable business, and sawmills replaced the rice fields. Historians found that ancestors of First Lady Michelle Obama had been enslaved on Friendfield Plantation, which was in Georgetown. Jim Robinson, Michelle Obama's great-great grandfather, was born in 1850 on this plantation, where up to two hundred slaves worked.

During antebellum times, Georgetown District and the South Carolina lowlands had the largest number of slaves brought into our country. The slaves on the plantations had to cut and burn the trees, dig ditches, install floodgates, and then plant and cultivate the rice fields, a complicated engineering and farming activity. After the Civil War, many freed slaves stayed in Georgetown and actually had an impact on the development of its leadership. Between 1867 and 1910, most of the businesses on the main street of Georgetown were owned by colored people. Later, these businesses moved out to the edges of town and were replaced with white proprietors.

Georgetown survived the collapse of the rice plantations and moved into the lumber business. But during the Depression, the local banks failed, and the Atlantic Coast Lumber Company closed its shops. Unemployment and poverty were unfortunate realities throughout the country, and Georgetown welcomed Franklin Delano Roosevelt's relief programs. I knew nothing of

Georgetown's early history and as a child didn't recognize the town as being beautiful. Perhaps the adults knew all of this, and the children were too busy with their day-to-day childish activities to recognize these attributes.

Even though employment improved when the paper mill moved in, racial discrepancies didn't. The mill had segregated restrooms and water fountains. Showers for their employees were provided but were also segregated. Even the windows where paychecks were picked up were segregated—the colored employees went to the colored window and the whites went to the white window. In the late 1940s, when an official came in to enforce better conditions for colored people, the showers and restrooms were enlarged and opened for everyone. Some of the whites were so upset that they just stopped using the showers and brought their own drinking water.

We heard stories about racial incidents in the area. One was about a colored man who was stabbed and lying on the sidewalk in a white neighborhood. People gathered around and debated whether to call a black ambulance or get the closest white ambulance. Was he helped? No one remembered or spoke about the outcome of this incident. Another story involved a colored man who was arrested while trying to vote. He was told that he couldn't vote because he had not paid his taxes, so he protested, was thrown in jail, then shot five times.

Schools, restaurants, and other establishments were segregated, and most whites seemed to think everything was fine. They voted for Strom Thurmond, who supported segregation. He served in the South Carolina Senate for five years, was a circuit judge for eight years, and served in the United States Senate for forty-eight years after that. In 1957 he gave the longest filibuster speech ever recorded to the United States Congress. He was protesting civil rights. It lasted twenty-four hours and eighteen minutes. He said in part of his speech, "There's not enough troops in the army to force the southern people to break down segregation and admit the nigger race into our theatres, into our swimming pools, into our homes and into our churches."

Georgetown's library was segregated. White people went to a small room in one of the old buildings in the white section of town. There were no real colored libraries with children's rooms and good selections of new books at that time, so these young children had only books the school provided. It seemed like my sister always had her head in a book and would have Mother take her to our white library each week. I had never been in the library and didn't have any books of my own, so I read stories out of the Book of Knowledge set that was in our living room or picked up and read any of my sister's old books that I could find. On one of the trips to the library, my sister asked if I could go in with her.

Mother asked, "Are children allowed to go in there? She's only five." I myself was terrified to go into that tall, mysterious red-brick building with vines growing all over its side. I don't remember the name of the book my sister checked out for me, but it had little red strawberries on the cover. I wish I had read more as a child, but I was occupied elsewhere.

There were several restaurants downtown, but we hardly ever went out to eat. One of the teenage drive-ins was the Whistling Pig, where you could buy the best chili dog in town. The Milk Bar was a favorite hangout for the white high school students. There kids would sit around drinking cherry Cokes and root beer. Once Mother had my sister take me in there after school to wait until she could pick us up. I was excited to see what went on in there, but my sister was mortified. I guess she didn't want to be bothered with a little sister in front of her friends. But she did order me a cherry Coke.

Saturdays in the little town of Georgetown were always busy. My parents usually went into town that day and would get up early so they could find a good parking place downtown. Parking meters had been installed on the streets, but you could park for free on weekends. People strolled along Front Street in small-town style and stopped to talk with friends. I loved to walk along the street with my mother and sister and look in the store windows. Ever since 1936, when the paper mill came into town and brought a degree of prosperity, new dress shops that had the latest fashions for ladies and hardware stores with all kinds of gadgets for men had opened their doors. My father would take me into Kaminski's Hardware Store. I loved the smell of grease and was amazed at the number of bins that contained all sizes of nails and screws. Since some merchandise was stored on shelves upstairs, the owner set up a miniature trolley that ran on a track near the high ceiling. If a customer wanted a special item that was upstairs, he called the stock boy, who would go up and load the item on the trolley and send it downstairs. I would watch at the bottom of the circular stair, hoping to get a glimpse of that trolley.

Right next to the hardware store was the old town clock building that was originally used as an open market we were told had been used to sell slaves. Mounted on a large sign were the words, "SLAVE MARKET." Someone told me that when you walked through the covered tunnel-like walk through the building you could hear the ghosts of slaves yelling and crying. When I went with my father to the hardware store and passed through there, I held his hand tightly, especially when I looked at the slave chain that was embedded in the wall.

Fogels was the fancy dress store in town. Its owner shopped all over the country to bring in the latest fashions for women. It was owned by one of the Jewish families who lived in the community. My sister said disapprovingly about that family, "I don't know why they close the store on Saturdays. And they don't read our Bible." This store was too fancy for us, so we just looked in the window. The owner of the Red Sox baseball team lived nearby, so Fogels would always have Red Sox signs all over the store, especially during baseball season.

My mother shopped at Alwyn's, the men's and ladies' ready-to-wear store. The building was long and narrow, with a front door and a back door and no windows. Ladies' fancy dresses, coats, and hats were on one side, and men's suits and felt hats on the other. Glass-covered showcases on the men's side held watches and personal items, while rhinestone pins and necklaces were displayed in covered cases on the women's side. Trousers, gloves, and other men's items were stacked on tables in the aisle that ran down the middle of the store. We were an all-white clientele. I never saw any colored people in these stores, and I never questioned, "Why?" That was just the way it was, and I accepted two styles of living in my town.

There were two movie houses on Front Street: the Palace, which opened in 1936 with the showing of Jean Harlow in *Libeled Lady,* and the Strand, which opened in 1941. Some Saturday afternoons my parents would give us twelve cents and let us go see the movie while they shopped. Lines of screaming children stood in front of the ticket window waiting for it to open. We watched Dale Evans and Roy Rogers and Gene Autry, but my favorites were Captain Marvel, Flash Gordon, and the Invisible Man. Popcorn was only ten cents, but I never had money for that. Of course, the theatre was segregated, but I never even noticed.

Most people got their paychecks on Fridays, so the women would go into town to buy groceries on Saturdays. The local A&P grocery store was always packed with white customers, while the colored people went to little groceries near the colored side of town. My sister and I would usually sit in the car and wait while our mother would do her weekly shopping. We didn't know that A&P stood for the Atlantic and Pacific, so we would laugh and say, "We're going to the A and pee." I did wonder if they had a bathroom in there.

As you drove into town, you had to cross over the railroad track before you came to the main part of the street with the parking meters. There were a lot of colored people at this spot, since this was where friends or relatives dropped them off for the day to shop. Some white people would set up tables on the edge of the street, hoping to attract colored people to their rummage sales. My teenage sister and her friends would often go there to sell hand-me-down or used items like old shoes, purses, clothes, chipped dishes, and pots and pans. Nothing was marked over twenty-five cents, but the going rate was usually ten cents. She would come home with about a dollar in change, which she would dangle in my face.

Once my best girlfriend and I decided we wanted to go downtown and make a dollar in the rummage economy. I climbed the rickety stairs that led to our attic and began going through old boxes of clothes and things that my mother had stored there. I found a few shirts that might do, even though they had some tears, a purse that had seen better days, and a pair of ladies' shoes. My mother donated a pot that had burn marks on the bottom and a toaster that she hadn't used in years. She looked at the items that I picked out and said I could have them, too. I showed her the purse that "had seen better days" and asked her if it would sell. She said, "It probably will because colored people won't know the difference anyway."

On Saturday morning my parents drove Kathleen and me to the end of Front Street near the railroad crossing. The streets were already busy and all the parking spots were full, so they let us out next to the curb. We set our table up under the shade of a mulberry tree and carefully arranged our items so the colored shoppers could see them. Within five minutes, several colored women came by. One woman bought a purse from Kathleen for twenty-five cents that was in a much better condition than the one that I had marked fifty cents.

Kathleen was a good seller and would step out and say, "Come look at what we have for sale." I decided that I should do the same and picked up the toaster I had on the table. A colored woman stopped, and trying to imitate Kathleen, I said, "Look at this toaster I have. It's only fifty cents." The woman looked straight in my face and asked, "How do I know it would even work?" She then pushed her way onto the sidewalk and disappeared. What was this? My mother told me colored people wouldn't know the difference between things that were good or those that were damaged, and here this woman had questioned my wares.

At the end of the day when my parents picked us up, Kathleen had made a dollar and I had made ten cents. I put my dime in my coin purse and wondered how this colored woman knew enough to ask if the toaster would work. Where did she learn this? Was this typical of colored people, or was she just the exception? Maybe she was one of those smart Yankee colored women I had heard about. They were smarter than ours. I never talked with Mother about this because I thought she had already made her opinion about colored people quite clear in this matter.

EENIE, MEENIE, MINEY, MOE: WHAT'S IN A NAME

The small town in South Carolina where I spent the first twelve years of my life was an idyllic place in which to grow up. I can only speak for myself, since I was in a middle-class, Christian, white family. What I later learned was that though most families in the United States had hardships during the Depression and the war, black families struggled racially as well as economically.

The entire culture was permeated with racial division and concepts of differences: principally, it centered around the inferiority of the descendants of these former slaves who were all around us. Over the years, names for people of color changed in my community. My grandparents referenced those with dark skin as "darkies" and called the little girls "pickaninnies." The adults that I knew used the term "colored people" but at times slipped and called them "coons," "negras," "niggras," "niggas," or "niggers." I had also heard colored people called "jungle bunnies," "jigaboos," "burrheads," and "tar babies."

I never heard my parents use those most derogatory words until I became an adult. It was then, when I was strongly questioning the old ways, that my father, irritated at my changes in thinking, called me a "nigger lover" and referred to colored people as "burrheads." If anything bothered my mother regarding the colored people, she would shrug, scrunch up her nose, and express her feeling by saying, "THOSE negras!"

The culture was soaked in its heritage of slavery. In elementary school, our teacher would take us into the lunchroom, where the music teacher led us in sing-a-longs. We sang songs like "Bicycle Built for Two," "Row, Row Your Boat," "Oh, Susannah," and "Polly Wolly Doodle," but my favorite was "Ol' Black Joe." Its lilting melody was accompanied by words that said, "I'm comin', I'm comin'/For my head is bending low./ I hear those gentle voices calling, Ol' Black Joe." I sang all of these with gusto, not wondering for a moment if some colored people would be offended by the underlying meaning of these folk songs. Perhaps they were so used to these descriptions that they were not offended but only sad, or even unnoticing, when they heard these lyrics about their enslaved ancestors. "That's just the way it is" ran both ways with some in both sides of our community, I believe.

Early on I had a real interest in music and found I had a "nice singing voice." I was interested in tuneful songs that I could sing, and the songs I mentioned by Stephen Foster were among the ones I loved. Stephen Foster was born in 1826 and became known as "The Father of American Music." He wrote parlor music and music for minstrel shows, where black-faced performers sang songs with dialects that depicted colored slaves as simple people. However, today it is said that Foster wanted white performers not to mock slaves but to perform his songs in a way that would encourage compassion for them. Even though some abolitionists frowned when they heard some of these lyrics, the songs continued to be sung in the parlors of American families.

If Foster did favor compassion towards the group, it wasn't always obvious. Foster's song, "Turkey in the Straw," was originally named "Zip Coon," and one verse of "Polly Wolly Doodle" said:

I came to a river an' I couldn't get across,
Sing Polly wolly doodle all the day.
So I jumped on a niggra', an' I tho't he was a horse,
Sing Polly wolly doodle all the day.

The second verse of "Oh, Susannah," which is never sung today, says,
I jump'd aboard the Telegraph
and trabbeled down de ribber
De lectric fluid magnified
and kill'd five hundred Nigger.

In Foster's song, "Massa's in the Cold, Cold Ground," the lyrics say,
Back in the cornfield, hear dat mournful sound
all de darkies am a weeping
Massa's in the cold, cold ground.

The words in "Old Uncle Ned" say,
Der was an old Nigger day called him Uncle Ned.
He's dead long ago, long ago!
He had no wool on de top ob his head
De place where do wool ought to grow.

"My Old Kentucky Home" is still used each year at the Kentucky Derby. The first verse says that the sun shines bright and the darkies are happy, while another verse says, "The head must bow and the back will have to bend, wherever the darkey may go..." Florida's state song is "Old Folks at Home," better known as "Way Down Upon the Suwanee River," where the lyrics say, "still longing for the old plantation and the old folks at home." So it was in my time in that small southern town.

Story time in first grade was wonderful. My teacher, Miss Crawford, had a magical voice that captured the words off the page and navigated them to our eager ears. "Little Black Sambo," written in 1899, was a popular story in our class. When Miss Crawford read, she turned the book so we could see the brightly colored pages. Sambo's clothes were colored in blues, purples, and reds, and the tigers, of course, were bright yellow with stripes. I don't think we noticed that Sambo had thick lips, fuzzy hair, and huge eyes. But I am sure we saw Sambo's black skin.

Miss Crawford certainly didn't tell us that the name Sambo in the eighteenth century was used to refer to those of mixed race and later in the nineteenth century began to mean a lazy African male. In the twentieth century, there was a chain of restaurants called Sambo's that displayed black, thick-lipped, fuzzy-haired boys on its signs. Later, the restaurant chain used only tigers on its signs.

At school recess, we played the regular games of dodgeball, pop the whip, jacks, hopscotch, and group sports like softball. At times we had to choose sides and would chant, "Eenie, meenie, miney, moe. Catch a nigger by his toe. If he hollers let him go. Eenie, meenie, miney, moe." I'm not sure if my friends and I realized the underlying meaning of this chant. I don't even remember knowing what a nigger was. That term was not used in my home at that time.

I always wanted to be an artist, but I wasn't very talented. The only drawing or artwork I did was coloring pictures in my coloring book. In school the teacher would pass out coloring sheets and eight basic, colored crayons. When we colored pictures of children, we would choose the crayon marked "white." There never were any colored children in my pictures, so

I didn't have to worry about using the black or brown crayon for people. I remember using the white crayon to color a girl and thinking, "That girl looks like a ghost. I hope I don't look like that." I took a red crayon and lightly covered the white girl in the picture. That didn't accomplish much because it looked like the girl was sunburned. It was one of the first times I really thought carefully about a person's skin color.

One night after supper I stretched out on the floor and flipped through the pages of my coloring book trying to decide which picture to color. I had already colored the pictures of trees and flowers and the only ones left were those with children playing together. I picked up my old cigar box of used crayons and began searching for the best one to color the children. I found white crayons and pink ones and red ones, but each of those didn't seem like the color of my skin. Carefully, I opened a new box of crayons that I'd just gotten and found one marked "peach." I thought this would be a good color for peaches and remembered someone calling pretty girls from Georgia, "Georgia Peaches." While thinking to myself, "This must be the color of the pretty Georgia girls' skin," I pulled the peach crayon out of the box and began filling in the children's faces with the new crayon. It still didn't look right, but at least the children weren't sunburned or ghosts.

The belittling terminology for blacks in our area grew as slowly for me as had recognition of skin color. Oddly, I can connect derogatory terms with specific times and happenings. Momie, my grandmother, lived in south Louisiana and would come up to stay with us for several weeks at a time. She was a petite Cajun lady with auburn hair and green eyes. At night she would kneel by the open window in my room and say her prayers. Then she would read to me and tell me stories about herself and my grandfather. It was always fun playing "Old Maid and "Go Fish" with her and my sister because she always let me win. During one of those stays, she went with my mother and Margaret into a colored neighborhood to take some clothes to a woman to be washed. That part of town was called shantytown. The sidewalks and paved streets always stopped when the white section of town ended; cars had to continue on rugged dirt roads. No matter how careful drivers were, dust would boil up from the bottom of the car and cover the seats with gray film.

When Mother stopped in front of a small unpainted house, my grandmother pointed to some children sitting on the porch and said, "Look at that little pickaninny with its hair all in braids." That day, my sister added that word to her vocabulary. She told me later this was the first time she remembered hearing the word "pickaninny."

In the mid-1940s, we got a call saying my grandfather was in the hospital in New Orleans. We packed clothes and snacks in our Ford car and began the trip to the big city. It was during a tropical storm, and the Louisiana roads near the bayous were covered with water. The swish of the windshield wipers lulled me to sleep, but I jumped up when my father shouted, "Look, there's an alligator in the road." He carefully maneuvered the car around the reptile, which continued to lie on the road.

Charity Hospital was built in 1939 and was supervised by the Catholic Sisters of Charity. On its completion, it was considered the second-largest hospital in the United States. We had visited Papa Jim in his room, and then it was decided I was to go with my grandmother to get something to eat. It was late afternoon, and she held my hand as we pushed through the crowd that was headed to the exit doors. There were doctors in white coats, nurses with little white caps, and all kinds of people rushing someplace. I stared at the nuns with long black dresses and white hats that covered their heads and draped down their shoulders. I clutched my grandmother's hand tighter since I was scared I'd get lost.

We finally came to the massive exit doors, pushed them open, and started down the steps when a colored man accidently bumped into Momie. She shouted, "Those darkies should watch where they are going!" I glanced up at her, trying to internalize this word. I had heard grown colored men called niggers or boys, but I had never heard them called "darkies" at that time except in songs. It sounded odd. I did know colored people never called a white person by his first name. They had to use the white person's last name, prefaced with Mr. or Mrs. or Miss. The white people just called the colored person by his or her first name.

Prejudice against colored people wasn't the only kind of negative thinking, of course. I never met any Native Americans, but in the movies they were always called names like "Injuns," "squaws," and "redskins." The Indians were often portrayed as threatening people who scalped the pioneers.

In school we sang the song "Ten Little Indian Boys" but pronounced it "Ten Little Injun Boys." At the end of the song the boys would get up and whoop and holler while they waved their arms in the air as if they had hatchets. The girls would take a squaw-like stance with arms folded over their chests, stomp around, and say, "Ugh, ugh."

There weren't many Jews in the little town of Georgetown, and I'd never even heard the word "Jew" when I was a young child. I remember one time hearing someone call another person "hymie" and "kike." I didn't know what that meant and thought it might have been his middle name. People usually didn't use their middle names, so I didn't think much about it.

Name-calling wasn't limited to a race or religion in my town. Anyone who didn't fit the normal standards could be singled out. I know this was not associated just with southern behavior, of course, and I do admit it may be part of human nature, if an ugly part. The big yellow school bus would pick me up at home and drop me off each morning at school. I was always early, so I'd walk to the side door and wait for the bell to ring. One cold winter morning as was I walking to the door I heard shouting and thumping noises. When I got closer I could see some children throwing rocks at a girl huddled under the overhang of the door. They were shouting horrible things —"white trash," "hillbilly," and "peckerwood." I knew what those words meant: poor white trash. The girl was one of my third-grade classmates but not one of my best friends. We never played together at recess, and I never even sat next to her in class. Still, this was not something people should do.

I pushed my way past the bullies and walked up to the steps where the little girl was standing, wearing a short cotton dress that barely covered her underpants and a thin sweater that was way too small. She didn't have any socks on, and her brown shoes were so worn that the toes were sticking out. I walked over and put my arm around her shoulder. Her hair was all greasy and matted. Yellow liquid dripped out of her nose then ran down the middle of her face onto her chin. As I got closer, I could see her pierced ears were infected and oozing with pus. Pieces of twine were pulled through the holes so they wouldn't grow back.

Hugging, I pulled her closer. I looked at the bullies and said, "If you hit her, then you will have to hit me. I'm going to stay here 'till you leave." I was one of the best students in the class and was always chosen for class leader and most favorite, so I hoped they might listen to me. As we stood huddled together in the frigid temperature, the bullies looked at each other, dropped the rocks, and left. I felt her skinny ribs and smelled her unwashed body, then pulled her closer to keep her warm. She was shivering not only from cold but probably from the humiliation she had gone through.

Even though I was popular in social situations, when we played team sports at recess, I was the last one chosen for a team because I was the least athletic. I knew what it was like to be chosen first and what it was like to be standing there alone. I never played with this poor little girl and never even talked with her after that day, but I was moved at her plight on that cold South Carolina morning in 1948.

As an adult, looking back at that young age, I wondered why I was beginning to see the inequalities around me. I asked myself, "Why does a child brought up one way in an area of certain cultural mores take on divergent views from parents and the neighborhood?" How much was taught at home, and how much in group situations? How much did the past affect the present?

Both of my parents were kind and knew fairness, even though it didn't extend to colored people. They were only victims of the culture in which they were brought up, and weren't able to escape. Meeting and living with other cultures in close situations can't help but be good. At that early age, I was never around any people of color and wasn't aware of the cultural negativity of being black.

My belief for fairness didn't come with a sudden overnight revelation. It came gradually first through my upbringing in the church. One of the very first verses I memorized was the Golden Rule, "Do unto others as you would have them do unto you." Another one was, "Love your neighbor as yourself." In my mind and heart, I felt whatever the Bible said was true, and I should try to live by its message.

At Christmas the teacher had us draw names for secret Santas. We didn't really care whose name we drew but worried about who drew our name. The teacher made us promise we would never reveal whose name we drew. I drew a boy's name, and my mother went to the dime store and bought a present for him. I wouldn't be seen buying a boy's toy. She wrapped the present and I tied a name card on the bow.

The last day before Christmas vacation, we took the presents to school and put them under the tree that was perched on a table in front of the class. We had decorated it with all kinds of paper ornaments and chains made out of macaroni that was strung on brown yarn. We thought it was beautiful. Even though we just sang songs and played games in the morning, it seemed like vacation was years away. Finally, lunch and recess was over and the last hour of the day arrived. It was time for the big present opening. The teacher picked up each present, called the name written on it, and motioned for the child to go up and get it. We had to wait until everyone got his or her present before we opened ours. She then said, "You may open your presents now."

Everyone yanked the bows off and ripped the paper to shreds as they tore it off the carefully wrapped presents. I could hear, "Wow!" and "What did you get?" and "This is nice." I looked at some of my girlfriends who were holding up little boxes of candy or miniature bottles of perfume or plastic bracelets. I pulled the paper off of my present only to find a small metal globe bank—an educational present. Since the presents didn't have the names on them saying who the presents were from, we didn't know who gave them to us. Later, we would ask each other in private, "Did you give me the present?" so in a roundabout way we found out who each secret Santa was.

I figured out that my secret Santa was the little girl whom I saved from the bullies. She was so poor that the teacher bought the present for her—a little globe bank. I still have this little bank today, and when I look at this token of love bought by my third-grade teacher in 1948 I wonder what happened to this little girl who had stood shivering in the cold. We children would often shout when we were called names or were verbally abused, "Sticks and stones may break my bones, but words will never hurt me."

But, sometimes words do hurt.

THE KLAN IN OUR NEIGHBORHOOD

The Ku Klux Klan organization had been studied and written about by so many authors, but the knowledge of that group was kept secret from most of the white children of my day in Georgetown. Colored children, though, had firsthand experiences with this intimidating group.

History writes that the Ku Klux Klan organized after the Civil War to use threats and violence against colored people to "keep them down." The members wore masks and robes to hide their identity during night raids. Some superstitious Negros thought these masked riders were ghosts of Confederate soldiers. In a way they might have been, because they carried on the bigoted dislike of blacks many Confederates had felt when they fought to preserve slavery. And rabble-rousing General Nathan Bedford Forrest was said to have been part of the Klan beginnings when he experienced the devastating end of "The War Between the States."

The Klan dwindled away toward the end of the 1800s but was replaced by other organizations. In 1874, the Red Shirts, a paramilitary group who disrupted elections and suppressed voting, was formed in South Carolina and helped its candidate win the gubernatorial race. It was said this political race was the bloodiest in South Carolina history at that time, with Negroes being sought out if they wished to vote and some killed. That the Klan operated openly and above board may be surprising to some. They remained active until the 1890s.

The Ku Klux Klan re-emerged in 1915 at Stone Mountain, Georgia, and spread throughout most of the states. The group focused on opposition toward Negros, Jews, Catholics, and immigrants. The release of the silent movie, *The Birth of a Nation*, reflected, and probably stimulated, the formation of the new Klan. This movie portrayed Negros as unintelligent and sexually aggressive toward white women. President Wilson had a private viewing of the film at the White House and said, "It's like writing history with lightning, and my only regret is that it is all so terribly true." The film caused riots in theatres and was censored in some cities.

Many historians believe the new Klan in the Midwest grew directly out of the wartime Confederate support group, the Copperheads, in states like Illinois, Ohio, and Indiana. Members of the Knights of the Golden Circle and the Order of American Knights just lay low for a while and reorganized as the Klan in midwestern states. These sub-rosa, culturally angry groups converged, at least in sentiment, in mid-America.

By the 1920s the Klan in the Midwest or West had many new members. It marketed itself as a family organization, trying to mask its more sinister purposes in gatherings like picnics and songfests. Almost one in five of Indiana's white male population was a member. Many people do not realize that the major hostility of the Klan during the 1920s was toward Catholics, with blacks a secondary target. Large numbers of Catholic immigrants had settled in northern Indiana and patronized the University of Notre Dame. These Catholics, taking jobs from lower-income groups with an older heritage, provoked local rage. In 1924, when the Ku Klux Klan had a meeting in the South Bend area, students from Notre Dame confronted them and stole some of the Klan emblems. It took the president of the university and its football coach Knute Rocke to convince the students to stay on campus to prevent further violence.

The northern members wore masks and robes as they had and still did in the South, then incorporated cross burnings and prayer into their ceremonies. The Klan was disrupted in the 1920s, and its power was smashed in the Midwest, when a group of right-minded Hoosiers brought justice to its leader, D.C. Stephenson. He was on trial in Noblesville, Indiana, for the sexual assault and murder of a statehouse worker named Madge Oberholtzer. A jury put Stephenson away for the rest of his life in 1925, and subsequent trials of Klan leaders ended its power. Stephenson was paroled in 1956 on the condition that he leave Indiana and never return.

But it can be said with truth that it was in the South that the most vitriolic, violent, and dangerous opposition to black citizenship occurred. Even though the membership of the KKK continued to plummet, many small groups used the name to oppose the civil rights movement and desegregation. Notorious murders, bombings, and other violent acts persevered. In 1948, two white women in our own Georgetown were raped and murdered. Residents whose anger was fueled by the Ku Klux Klan organized a lynch mob to hang a man who had not even come to trial. The suspect was a colored war veteran. The only evidence that convicted him was a scar on his face. The situation became so intense that the governor of the South Carolina had to call in the state militia to prevent more violence.

Adults in my childhood community knew there was "trouble," as they called it, from time to time around "uppity blacks," or those who sought rights they believed were theirs as a result of law and decency. Jews, and to a lesser extent Catholics, were still in the lens of disruptive prejudice around us. Bernard Baruch, the wealthy Wall Street financier who purchased plantations around Georgetown, hosted presidents, prime ministers from other countries, and politicians to hunt and fish on his Hobcaw Plantation. In 1951, Ku Klux Klan members met in conclave near Baruch's plantation, and the leader railed against him as a Zionist Jew. The leader also said the colored people were using extensive propaganda in an attempt to end segregation. That night the Ku Klux Klan members didn't wear the typical sheets they usually did at rallies, but the crowd was just as intense. My parents never talked about these happenings around me. That was their world and not mine.

But let us return to the time when I was in grade school. In the late 1940s, my mother was a stay-at-home mother and my sister was in school. My father worked on different shifts at the paper mill. Some days he had the 7AM to 5PM shift or the 5PM to midnight shift, and at other times he had the dreaded graveyard shift from midnight to 7AM.

When he was on the graveyard shift, he had to sleep during the day, so he would go to the large attic, turn on a big window fan and try to sleep. On those days we had to be very quiet so we wouldn't disturb him. Before he left for work that night, he would check his metal lunch box and make sure his thermos bottle was filled with coffee. My mother would usually place a tin of Vienna sausage or sardines with a packet of saltine crackers in the black lunch box in case he got hungry. When he was on the day shift, he would drive the two miles home from the mill for his lunch and take a short nap before he went back to work. People often smiled and said, "The paper mill closes down each day at noon so the workers can go home to eat."

It was during one of his day shift schedules when I heard him pull up in the driveway a few minutes after noon. Instead of stopping on the porch to take his shoes off like he usually did, he rushed into the kitchen and quietly began to discuss something with my mother. This led to questions from my mother, who kept looking over her shoulder at me as if she were trying to keep the subject a secret. We sat down and ate lunch at the kitchen table like we always did, but instead of my mother washing the dishes right away and my father taking a quick nap before going back to work, he loaded my mother and me into our little Ford car.

I thought, "This might be something special." If something was going on, my father wasn't going to let it go uninvestigated. He was as curious as anyone I ever knew. My father Bernie was born in Morgan City, Louisiana, in 1910. His family wasn't wealthy but instilled in him and his only brother the need for an education. He attended Louisiana State University for two years, then went to an electrical school in Chicago. Daddy was always interested in everything. Once, when I kept asking question after question like, "Why is the sky blue?" or "How do birds fly?," my mother finally gave up and said, "When you get to heaven, you can ask God." That night I prayed to God, "When I get to heaven, please remind me to ask you all those questions."

We didn't have television in those days, so my father would come home from work with interesting things to tell us. One night he took my sister and me out in the front yard and pointed to the sky. He said something about the alignment of the stars and how that would not happen again in many years. We watched lunar eclipses from start to finish and watched a solar eclipse once by gazing at the sun through a brown camera negative. He would take us to historical places in Charleston and tell us stories about them. When we visited his parents in southern Louisiana, he took us to a nearby icehouse to show us how ice was made and delivered to houses. Everything was something to be explored.

So, on this day, as we rode in the car out in the country without even washing the dishes, I knew something was up. Lunch tried to settle in my stomach while I held on to the window knob on the back seat. I kept my neck turned as I looked out the side window, trying to see where my father was taking us. My parents weren't saying a word as the car bumped along the road, but I could feel the tension in the car. These were days when gas was rationed, and we never went for "joy rides" except on Sundays after church.

The country road was gravel, and dust billowed up as my father drove the car slowly, hoping no rocks would bounce up and break a window. We rode past our church and then turned off the gravel road toward a group of houses that were built before our house was. This was the route my school bus took each day, but I didn't know many of the children who lived in these houses. However, my parents seemed to know the families in this area.

My father stopped the old Ford in front of a house. I knew it; I always thought this house was beautiful with its brick front and nice yard. It had a large chimney, and at Christmas the owners decorated it with lights and put a Santa on the roof. "Why are we stopping?" I asked. "Did someone die?" Still no answer. The motor on the car kept running, and I thought my father was going to turn it off to save gas like he always did, but he didn't. My mother turned and stared past my father onto the large lawn of the house. She let out a quiet murmur to my father, "Where is it?" My father pointed to the edge of the house where a pile of burned wood was lying.

I saw ashes but didn't understand what had happened. Had the house caught on fire, or had the owners had a giant wiener roast? Then I heard my mother ask, "Did they wear sheets?" What was she talking about? The only time I had heard anyone talking about wearing sheets was at Halloween, when we draped sheets over our heads and went trick or treating disguised as ghosts. Or—I remembered the time I got tangled in the sheets that were hanging on the clothesline outside our house to dry. On what we called "Wash Day Monday," my mother would put our dirty bedsheets in the bathroom tub, and my sister and I would take turns stomping on them to get the dirt out. After the sheets soaked for a few hours, she would rinse them and take them out in the backyard, clipping them on the clothesline with wooden clothespins. One Monday morning I was running through the yard and took a shortcut through the wet clothes. I knocked the pole down that was holding the line up, and everything came falling down on me. I could hardly breathe, but somehow I got untangled. As quickly as I could, I grabbed the clothesline and propped it up with the pole, hoping my mother hadn't seen me.

So sheets served purposes mostly connected with beds. Then why was anyone wearing them at this house out here? I couldn't hear my father's answer to my mother's question, but their muted tones suggested something bad must had happened. My father looked at his wristwatch and said, "We better hurry. I don't want to be late for work." He turned the brown Ford around and sped back to our house. When he turned into the driveway, he didn't turn the motor off, so my mother and I slid out the door and waved goodbye as he left.

When we went inside, I asked my mother what had happened, but the only thing she said was, "Nothing. Just don't talk about it to anybody." I didn't mention it to anyone but always wondered if someone in sheets might come to our house and have a wiener roast on our lawn. Later, I heard what had happened. Someone at work had told Daddy there had been a cross burning in a yard near our house. Since there were no colored people living in this part of town, the targeted person must have been a Jew, Catholic, or someone who sided with a colored person. When Daddy was talking to Mother, he seemed as if he knew the owners, but I never heard him say a name.

A police officer lived in that house at the time of the 1948 rape/murder incident. Was he one of the officers who protected the colored man from the lynch mob? Were there other cross burnings at that time in Georgetown that were related to this same incident? I never found out, and no detailed records exist. Men in those days often had to look the other way when injustice reared its head. I don't think my father was a member of the Klan. However, I do know he must have been afraid this trouble might spread and his family would be tangled up in the mess. That is why he took Mother and me to see the place and the ashes of the burning cross. Life went on in this town and, like all towns, it kept its secrets hidden until time healed the hurt of those who suffered injustices—or it didn't.

THE ACCIDENT

We would often travel to Charleston, which was about sixty miles from my town, Georgetown. Highway 17, a two-lane road that always needed repairs, took us all the way there, but before you reached the city itself you had to go over the Cooper River Bridge, which had been built in 1929. The two-lane bridge was ten feet wide with no medians or curbs. I was so terrified when we drove over the bridge that I would sit on the floor with my eyes closed.

Charleston was one of the oldest towns in America, and we were vaguely aware of its heritage. In the 1600s, Charleston was known as Charles Towne, named for King Charles II. The early economy was based on the deerskin trade, and soon the affluent plantation owners were using slaves to work their tea and rice fields. Charleston was often called "Holy City" because of the large number of churches in the city. These we were aware of when we drove through its streets.

Later I realized the city, with its stately buildings, had its own nationally known history and traditions. The Dock Street Theatre was the first theatre in the country; George Gershwin's opera *Porgy and Bess* was set in Charleston; sea captains would announce their arrival by putting a pineapple outside their door; the first game of golf was played in Charleston; before his famous invention, Samuel Morse painted portraits in the city; the first museum in the country was in Charleston; and finally, the Charleston Eagles, protected by officials, were the buzzards that cleaned up the meat scraps at the old city market.

In 1946, a ten-thousand-pound freighter rammed into the bridge we had to cross and ripped out a two-hundred-foot section, causing an entire family to fall into the water and drown. That was surely why I was so afraid to cross it. I remember how the traffic was backed up when they were repairing the bridge, and I would ask my parents, "Where did the car fall into the water?"

When we got into the city, we would pass antebellum houses with iron fences and lush gardens. There was one we called the Pink House that had plants in the yard with big pink and green leaves. My mother said they were caladium-like plants that were called elephant ears. I thought that was a perfect name for them. Every time we went to the city, my experience-hungry daddy would take us to at least one historical site. We went to the City Market, where slaves used to go to buy meat, fish, vegetables, and other food for the plantations and homes in the area. Nearby was the slave market building where slaves were held in jails before they were auctioned. Once we ventured out to Battery Promenade and the waterfront part of town. There was Middleton Place, where Arthur Middleton, a signer of the Declaration of Independence, lived. One Fourth of July night my father drove us to Charleston to watch the fireworks and celebration. The event was at the Charleston Harbor across from the remains of the Fort Sumter. On the drive there he tried to explain what happened during the Civil War at that fort. I was too excited to remember what the war was about, but the fireworks were wonderful to watch.

My mother and sister loved to buy things in Charleston, so my father would take me to the city park while they shopped. He would pay for peanuts so I could feed the birds and squirrels. Then he would sit on one of the benches near the water fountain and watch me entice the squirrels to eat out of my hand. One time he found a passing carnival near the park that had all kinds of attractions. He asked, "Do you want to ride on the Ferris wheel or the carousel?" I pointed to my choice, which was not the Ferris wheel or the carousel, then he handed a coin to the attendant and lifted me into one of the seats of the scariest looking ride, the Octopus. I shouted over the noise of the machine, "This is wonderful! It's better than shopping!"

One Saturday, Mother decided to take my sister and one of her friends to spend the day shopping in Charleston. Daddy was working, so she was going to drop me off at my Aunt Christine and Uncle Garland's apartment. Christine was the much-younger sister of my mother, and after their mother died, she had come to live with us for a while until she got married.

Mother and Christine loved the movies and would talk about the latest stars and their affairs. On one occasion I heard them talking about Lena Horne, a colored singer and actress. The discussion shed a lot of light on the beliefs of their generation in that part of the South. I didn't know anything about Lena Horne, but I was fascinated by their discussion. Christine asked, "Do you think Lena Horne is colored? Her skin isn't that dark." "I heard her mother was colored and her father was white," Mother answered. Christine continued, "She could certainly pass for white."

Then Mother said, "You know if you have one drop of colored blood in you, then you are colored." I wondered what she meant. I looked at my arm and wondered how you could find one drop of blood. Where would it be? Couldn't Lena Horne just suck it out, and then she would be a white person? Other times I heard them talk about the "Negras." They seemed to be glad that they didn't have to sit next to them at the movie house. Both of them agreed it was a good thing the colored people didn't go to the same school as my sister. Mother then commented, "You know they are just one jump out of the trees." All of this was confusing to me, and I wondered why colored people would be in trees anyway.

Anyway, on this particular occasion, I was excited about staying with Christine that Saturday while Mother went shopping. As soon as Mother stopped the car at Christine's, I jumped out and ran up the steps without even waving goodbye. Christine was fun to be with. She acted more like a teenager than a married aunt. She would let me put on her clothes and high heels and parade around the room like I was a movie star. I loved it when she showed me how to put on rouge and lipstick. She had all kinds of beauty tools stored in her dresser drawer. Once, I asked her to show me how to use an eyelash curler. After a demonstration, she said that I could curl her eyelashes. I put my fingers through the loops of the handle and placed the curler over one of her eyes then pulled the handle down as hard as I could. She let out such a yell that I thought the neighbors would come running over to see what had happened. Instead of clamping the curler on the eyelashes, I had clamped it on the eyelid itself. My poor aunt's eye swelled up so big it looked like someone had poked her with a hot stick. Luckily, she did forgive me.

Christine and Uncle Garland had been married for only a short time and lived in a two-room apartment over a garage in Georgetown. They didn't have much furniture, but she owned a big fluffy bed covered with a pale pink comforter that felt like pure silk. On the bedside table Christine had a little white radio with a lighted dial that was always set to the music station. She kept the volume turned all the way up, but you could still hear her beautiful voice over the music when she sang.

That evening my father and Uncle Garland were on the night shift at the paper mill and Christine and I were alone, lying on that fluffy bed, singing along with the radio. She turned the pages in her Hit Parade magazine and looked for the words to the songs that were being played. They might have been Perry Como's "Prisoner of Love" or Frank Sinatra's "Five Minutes More." Aunt Christine loved Frank Sinatra. Time passed. It was about midnight when she looked at the clock and said, "Why aren't they home yet? Dollie said they would be home before dark. They are way late." Christine began pacing the floor. She and Garland didn't have a telephone, so Christine looked at me and said, "I wonder if I should go to the neighbors and call Garland at work to see if something happened."

The next thing we heard was someone running up the stairs. The door pushed open and Uncle Garland rushed in. Christine knew he was home early, then saw the panicked look on his face. She hesitantly asked, "What's the matter? What happened?" Uncle Garland went to the closet and pulled out his shotgun. "Dollie hit a colored girl and the niggers are all around the car. Bernie is already on the way over there."

Hit a colored girl! Niggers around my Mother's car? What would happen? This was in the late 1940s, and there was a lot of anger and tension in Georgetown as well as all over the South. Many southerners had become afraid of colored people. The quiet, mumbling, and hat-holding men of the past were holding their heads up, proud, many of them of having served in World War II. A new spirit of growth and change was in the air, and jobs were beginning to open up to blacks in America. Many had headed north for real opportunity. Some black people were getting an education.

These moves in the South were not welcomed, and, as blacks began to rise in the pecking order just a bit, people around my town began to be even more vocal in their prejudiced opinions of why the coloreds shouldn't do that. Now I was old enough to hear the dictums, views, and strong opinions of white people around me. Colored men were more sexually aggressive than white men and would rape white women whenever they got the chance. Colored people around us would surely retaliate someday for what the slave owners had done to them or what they might think whites were doing to them now. No matter how you might educate them, as some were calling for, they would always be inferior. So it went.

Society realized by this time that the constant denigration and scorn of the years since the Civil War would not always be tolerated. In muted whispers, groups of whites were beginning to wonder what might happen "if they ever get the upper hand." These same white people didn't wish to even acknowledge the vicious and offensive acts the white slave owners did to their black slaves or the permanent underclass society had designated blacks should live in. The view of the plantation system was of beautiful pillared mansions, contented slaves by nice little cottages shelling peas, and the hum of soft music in the background. The beginning of *Gone with the Wind*.

That memorable night, I got out of the bed and sat at the kitchen table with Christine, numbed and confused at Uncle Garland's news. I was old enough now to understand their tone of worry and the broad outlines of the trouble. Something ominous might follow. We watched as Garland put on his hunting jacket, pulled a hat over his head, then left with his shotgun. Somehow the sheriff had notified him and my father at work. I wondered if Daddy took his shotgun, too. They must have been panicked when they heard colored people were gathered around this white woman's car that held my mother, sister, and her friend!

I slept at Christine's that night and heard the account of the accident the next day: It was dusk as Mother had been driving on the way back home from Charleston. My sister was in the front seat reading, and her friend was in the back seat. They had just approached the town of McClellanville, halfway between Charleston and Georgetown. This was a little fishing village with wooden houses tucked off in the moss-covered trees; about one thousand people lived there. As Mother drove into the town, traffic picked up, and she noticed bright lights were turned on in a field where a baseball game was starting. People stood on the edge of the field and sat in bleachers to watch the game. Cars and trucks had double parked along both sides of the road, leaving only a little space for cars to go through. The road was clogged and difficult to either see or to drive on. A six-year-old colored girl suddenly darted out into the highway in front of Mother's car. Mother couldn't stop in time and hit and killed the little girl. With the sound of impact, colored people began running across the field, onto the road, and gathered around the car. Someone must have called the sheriff, who took Mother, my sister, and her friend to a house and questioned them.

My sister said an officer interviewed her. He asked, "How fast was your mother driving?" She told him she didn't know, then he suggested, "Why don't we just say twenty-five miles an hour?" My father and Uncle Garland showed up with their hunting guns, then followed the car home as my fourteen-year-old sister drove; Mother wasn't up to it. She was, in fact, hysterical when a friend came to console her a few days later. I stood in the doorway of the living room and heard her say, "I still see the accident. I relive it. At night the little colored girl comes to me in a white dress. She talks to me..." I didn't understand the rest because Mother was crying uncontrollably.

The very next day after the accident, the Florence newspaper printed, "Dollie L. Overhultz swerved her car to miss a six-year-old girl that ran across the highway in McClellanville." Did she swerve? I didn't recall that being said. "No charges were filed." The sheriff had done his job. And after all, cars sometimes cannot avoid hitting someone who darts into the street. That's the honest truth of it.

If it had been the other way around, a colored person hitting a white girl, would the outcome have been different? Would there have been a trial? Would the colored driver have been allowed to leave the scene of the accident and go home? Would someone call the sheriff, or would mob mentality have taken over? Some white people probably would have thought, "The driver is just a colored person who doesn't know how to drive and should be punished," or "He was probably drunk like all colored people are on Saturday nights."

I cried and thought about how sad the little colored girl's family must be. But my mother was sad, too. She was a good woman who had accidently killed someone. Fatal accidents affect so many people, whites as well as those of color, caught up in a web of accusations, recriminations, and pain that lasted a lifetime.

ROPER HOSPITAL AND THE AUTOGRAPH BOOK

One of my best friends was Angela, who lived down the dirt road across from my house. It was 1950, and my playmates and I would ride our bikes up and down the road without a care, but we never ventured into that swampy area at the end of the road. Swarms of mosquitoes in this swamp were so thick that if you didn't pinch your nose, they would fly right up it. Snakes were all over in that morass, and there were rumors of alligators that would grab you and pull you underneath the algae-covered water. My sister told me she never went down there because she could hear ghosts wailing and moaning in the bug-infested swamp. When we were grown up, she admitted, "I was trying to scare you. It was just noise from cows that were being slaughtered."

Angela and her sister would come to my house and play dolls and dress-up. My mother had boxes of old clothes, shoes, hats, purses, and leftover sewing material in the attic. We would climb up the stairs and rummage through the boxes to see if we could find the right thing to dress up in. Each of us would take turns waltzing around the hot, musty attic as if we were models. When it got too hot, we would go outside and pretend we were going to town.

Angela was having a party for her tenth birthday. My mother and I had gone to the dime store and picked out a coloring book that I knew she would like. That afternoon, I watched Mother fold the pink tissue paper over the coloring book, tie a ribbon around it, and pull the extra string with the edge of the scissors to make it curl up like little pigs' tails. She handed it to me, and I carefully wrote in my best handwriting, "Happy Birthday. From Lou Ellen." I ran out the kitchen door, pushed the picket fence gate open, and darted across the gravel road. Dust flew in the air as I skipped toward Angela's house. There wasn't a thought in my mind except the anticipation of birthday cake and games—then an excruciating pain hit my head. I stumbled and looked around thinking someone had hit me with a rock. But no rock was there, or anything else. The pain over my eye was so intense that I nearly fell down. I couldn't see out of one eye, but I was almost at Angela's house.

I staggered on down the road like a drunk person and struggled up the steps to Angela's front door. Her mother opened the door and pointed to an empty chair. Everyone was seated in a circle and was playing "Hide the Thimble." They had their hands clasped in front of them and tried to pass the sewing thimble to the next person without being caught by "it" who was standing in the middle of the circle. I was trying to play, but when the thimble came to me I couldn't lift my hand to pass it on to the next person. I told Angela that I had a headache and wanted to go home. Her mother offered me an aspirin, but when she realized the intense pain I was in, she put me in her car and drove me to my house.

When my mother saw the car drive up, she rushed out to see what was wrong. I couldn't raise my hand to open the door, and I felt like I was going to fall down, so Mother took me out of the car and put me in her big bed, where I lay unconscious. I don't know how long it was before she called the doctor. Dr. Assey and his parents were from Syria. He was a big man with light brown skin and coal black hair. He was my family's doctor and had seen me ever since I was a baby. He had given me my smallpox shot, taken warts off my knees, sewn gashes on my legs, and treated burns on my arm. In those days, doctors still made house calls, so when my mother phoned his office, he came to the house and gave her some "smelling salts" wrapped in a cloth. He told her to hold them under my nose to keep me awake and he would come out the next day.

Mother must have been frantic because she couldn't keep me awake like Dr. Assey had instructed, so she called a new doctor in town, who came out immediately. After one quick look he put my mother and me in the back seat of his own car and drove us to Roper Hospital in Charleston.

Georgetown didn't have a hospital or any ambulance services at that time, and the closet treatment centers were over sixty miles away in Florence and Charleston. Roper Hospital in Charleston was one of the best-recognized teaching hospitals in the country at that time. Some people say medical students scrambled to attend medical school there because the hospital had one of the best facilities and most highly trained teacher staff in the country. It was keeping up to date in a time when medicine, following World War II, was undergoing radical change.

That venerable hospital had gone through many phases and expansions.

As a first facility, it opened in 1850 to treat "lunatics" and the poor. During the Civil War, it served as a Confederate hospital and a prison for Union soldiers. Later, it was wrecked by the 1886 earthquake. A second Roper Hospital was opened in 1906 and a third one in 1946, continuing to this day with a variety of names and combined resources and with Catholic management.

I seemed to have what was a concussion or other serious brain injury and needed to remain in the hospital. No diagnosis had been made at that time; something had happened in my brain, and they were working to know the cause. My small room in the hospital was on a corner in the newest building. During my coherent moments, I could hear carts rolling down the hall, doctors issuing orders, and visitors shuffling into loved ones' rooms. Each morning student doctors carrying charts and clipboards were escorted into my room and were given lectures about the patient...me.

One night I heard a child in one of the rooms screaming and some woman trying to comfort her. The next morning I asked my mother who was crying down the hall. She told me it was a little girl whose nightgown had caught on fire from a candle she was carrying. She was in terrible pain. Mother shook her head and wiped tears from her eyes.

Mother must have slept in a chair next to my bed while my father drove to the hospital each day after work. My father was in the waiting room late one afternoon when one of the doctors approached him. He told Daddy that I was diagnosed with a cerebral aneurysm, and if the bleeding didn't stop in the next few days, he would have to operate. He said it was rare for children to have this type of aneurysm, and if they did, they probably wouldn't survive.

Various spinal taps and other tests were performed while the doctors waited for the bleeding to stop. After several days of my slipping in and out of consciousness, a miracle happened and the bleeding stopped. My headache was gone, and I was allowed to get out of bed. The doctors still came into my room each morning and stared at me. Then they would step outside the door and talk about the recovery that had happened. But it was several days before I went home.

Someone in the hospital gave me an autograph book. It was maroon and about four inches by six inches. Printed on the cover were gold-colored words that said, "AUTOGRAPHS." One of the fads of the day was signing autograph books. This one was special because it was a real book; I usually made my own autograph books by folding papers together and writing "AUTOGRAPHS" on its cover.

In my little homemade autograph book at school, my friends had signed and I reciprocated with their books. Everyone passed the books around and sometimes looked for important people to sign them. Small-town celebrities, if you could get them, usually wrote in black ink, "It was nice meeting you," but friends would write verses or smart aleck remarks with a number 2 pencil, "Roses are red, violets are blue, sugar is sweet, and so are you." Someone might also say, "I know who your sweetheart is." Strangers often just signed their names.

In the days before I left the hospital, I asked everyone who came into the room to sign my book. Some doctors only signed their names, some wrote, "It was nice meeting you," but one wrote, "To my sweetest patient." Doctors signed, nurses signed, visitors signed, as well as other patients on the hall. I was elated.

One morning while my parents were outside the room talking with the doctors, an old gray-headed colored woman in a faded brown dress came in. She was hunched over and moved slowly as if she had a sore back. A metal bucket filled with smelly water clanked when she pushed it through the door. Without a word she picked up a dirty looking string mop and began cleaning the floor. As she came to the side of the bed, I caught her eye and said, "Would you sign my autograph book?" I held it up so she could see my prized book. She stopped, put the mop in the bucket, and raced out of the room. I was puzzled and asked myself, "What did I do?"

My parents came into the room right away, and Mother asked, "What did you say to that woman? She was crying." "I only asked her to sign my autograph book." My mother looked at my father, shook her head, and said to me, "She probably doesn't even know how to write."

A few days later, the colored cleaning woman stopped at the door of my room. She hesitated, and I gave her a little wave. She wasn't pushing the mop and bucket and looked a little different. Her faded brown dress was replaced with a clean navy one and a little flat hat was pinned to her head. Maybe she had dressed up for some occasion. She inched to the side of my bed and said, "I'll sign your book now." I gave her a pencil, opened the book, and pointed to a spot on a page. She took the book into her hands and with slow, jerky movements signed, "Mary Brown." I never saw her again. My mother watched her leave and said, "I bet she went home and practiced writing her name." I didn't think this was a big deal, but it may have been for Mary Brown, because now she had confidence to write her name.

After a few weeks, I was able to go home. The doctors and nurses waved at me as my parents put me in the car and drove me home to Georgetown and to my own feather bed. Several of my parents' friends came to visit and brought their children, who talked with me. My fourth-grade teacher even came to visit and brought me a book of paper dolls to cut out and play with. I settled back into my regular routine of school and church eventually, but my parents watched me with eagle eyes hoping and praying my recovery was permanent.

Two months later my father drove us to Charleston and took me to the doctor at Roper Hospital. My mother insisted Daddy take me by himself; she and my sister wanted to go shopping. We were ushered into the doctor's office. He smiled at me and talked with my father for a while. I didn't understand what he said, but it seemed like it was about how severe and unusual my condition had been. He gave Daddy a copy of a medical magazine that he had written an article for. "The article," he said, "explains Lou Ellen's spontaneous recovery from a pediatric cerebral aneurysm." He kept smiling at me, and I hoped he had signed my autograph book.

I took my maroon autograph book to school and had friends sign their variants on the "Roses are red, violets are blue" saying in it. We always tried to write more clever words than our friends in the books: "Yours till the Mississippi wears rubber pants to keep its bottom dry"; "Yours till butterflies"; "Roses are red, stems are green. You've got a figure like a submarine"; "Rose are red, violets are blue. I've got a bulldog that looks just like you." My boyfriend of that week signed, "Apples on the table, peaches on the shelf. Honey, I'm tired of sleeping by myself," and "When you get old and out of shape buy yourself a girdle for $2.98."

Another boy signed, "Butter to butter, cheese to cheese, what's a kiss without a squeeze?" then "I love you once, I love you twice. I love you better than chicken and rice."

I even guided a pencil that I held in my favorite black cat's paw and wrote, "Inkey."

There, among the signatures and sayings of my friends, doctors, nurses, and important people was the signature of Mary Brown. What was it that prompted me to ask this colored lady to sign my book? Why didn't I cringe at the thought of a colored person touching my book and pencil? What made me feel that Mary Brown was important?

I remembered lying in my Dixie Feather Hospital Bed in segregated Charleston and watching her cry. It was a glimpse of what colored people must have felt when they weren't recognized until they could write their own names, and that was a skill beyond them.

US HIGHWAY 17 AND THE GULLAHS

The old Charleston highway was a two-lane road in the 1940s with no lines down the middle or markings on the side. Cars crept along at a slow speed, being especially careful when they passed the logging trucks that could take over the entire road. Early morning fog on the wet swamps often snaked onto the road and dared any vehicle to go over 30 miles an hour. Crossing some of the wooden-planked bridges over the marsh-lined rivers was nerve-racking to the drivers as well as the passengers. The drivers called these bridges "knuckle breakers" because they held on to the steering wheel so tightly their knuckles turned white while maneuvering the cars over the planks.

Occasionally, as I've said, my parents would take trips to Charleston to shop, go to the dentist, or go to special events. I was always in the back seat of the car when we went, and to me as a child, the miles of pine trees lining the road through the Frances Marion National Forest seemed to go on forever. My sister would read, but I just sat and stared out of the window entertaining myself by making up stories in my head.

Once in a while, a farm community of colored people would pop up out of the forest. I would watch what was going on with interest as our car moved quickly by. There were colored people working in their gardens, sweeping the porches of their unpainted wooden houses, and plowing the fields with black mules. Their tilted houses had dirt paths that led to outhouses in the back. Colored women were putting wet clothes on the line while small children played in the dirt next to them. And then they were gone, as the car zipped on.

My father, I have to say, would slow down when we came to one of these populated areas. He wanted to be extra cautious after the disastrous accident with Mother's car. On one of these trips, I happened to see a colored girl sitting on the steps of her house clutching a white cat. It was such a contrast to see a black figure holding a white cat and probably loving it without thinking of its color. I thought about my black cat, Inkey, whom I deeply loved. My girlfriend and I would dress our cats up in doll clothes and pretend they were our babies. When we played dress-up, on the other hand, we would drape them over our shoulders and act like they were fur coats. My friend's cat didn't seem to mind this, but my cat Inkey wasn't as cooperative. I wondered if colored girls dressed their cats up in this same kind of torturing costume.

There were many plantations off US 17. My parents and I never visited them, but we could see arrows and signs that pointed to the roads that led to them. I was beginning to be aware of, and interested in, the history of our region. We were told the rice plantations of nearby Georgetown had been the largest producers of rice in the entire country and had hundreds of slaves. Wealth in the antebellum South was measured in the number of slaves you owned rather than the amount of land you had. If a plantation had over twenty slaves, then the owner was called a planter. These plantations we passed along US 17 definitely had had more than twenty slaves, so the owners were proud to be called planters.

Doing research recently, I found that one of these spreads Mother and Daddy mentioned, the Hampton Plantation, was built in 1735 and was one of the plantations in which George Washington stayed during his America tour through the South. The present owners still allow descendants of any slave who lived there to visit the old Gullah lot named Sam Hill Cemetery.

Another plantation I heard about as a child was the Hopsewee Plantation. It was built about 1740 by Thomas Lynch, Jr., one of the signers of the Declaration of Independence. Hopsewee was a major rice producer and in 1850 produced 566,000 pounds of rice on 240 acres with slave labor only. During the Civil War, the Union army looted the plantation and took what it wanted, then gave the rest to the slaves. Most of the slaves remained on the plantation as free people, but never grew rice again.

Farther down the road was a community that was shrouded in mystery and folklore. My sister and her friends told me that voodoo was practiced there by the colored people. My sister said, "If you look real close through the trees and hanging moss, you can see gray shacks with blood smeared across the doors to ward off any evil spirits." Some people said the voodoo priests there, like those of the past, would still pound on drums to send messages across the swamp. When we drove past this area, I would roll down my window and stick my head out to listen for drumbeats. I never heard any drums or saw any shacks, but I believed what I was told.

As an adult, I revisited the area and learned about its history and the Gullah dialect and culture these African American people preserved. Early in our country's settlement days in the South, Africans were captured and brought to the coastal areas. These captives came from different parts of western Africa and had different languages. After some time they combined their languages with some English, and the dialect they spoke became known as the Gullah language.

There are long lists of Gullah proverbs that have been translated into English: "Old firewood is not hard to rekindle," "Death is one ditch you cannot jump," "No matter how you try to cover up smoke, it must come out," "A burned child fears fire," "The heart doesn't mean everything the mouth says," "I've been in sorrow's kitchen and licked out all the pots." One proverb says, "Mus tek cyear ade root fa heal de tree." In translation it reads, "You need to take care of the root in order to heal the tree."

Song, dance, and prayer were included in the Gullahs' worship. Often the enslaved Africans would have worship services at midnight in the woods called "Howling Wilderness." The women and children went to the "praying ground" first, and the men followed with branches tied to their feet to hide any footprints. These meetings had to be very secretive since worship and unauthorized travel were banned. The Gullahs practiced witchcraft and voodoo, called juju or wadu. There were all kinds of remedies to help folks and all kinds of curses to hurt people. The root doctors were individuals who gave advice and protected others from curses and spells.

My parents had heard about these practices and customs but passed it off as just something the superstitious colored people did. There were no roads going down into these areas and the only access was by foot. Even if there had been roads, most whites would not have gone there because they were afraid of the idea of colored people practicing voodoo. The only contact most white people had with them was when they stopped at the lean-to shelters along the road where the Gullahs sold shrimp or raw oysters, which were stuffed into burlap bags for customers to take home.

People in Georgetown talked about some of the customs they believed these mysterious people practiced. One custom was to pass a baby over the coffin of a dead person to keep the spirit from coming back to haunt you. Another one was to carry an alligator tooth around in a pouch and feed it liquor, so it would bring you good luck in gambling activities. Still another was to gather goofer dust, which was graveyard dirt mixed with sand, the graveyard dirt captured right above a dead person's body just before midnight. If you sprinkled it over your property, evil wouldn't bother you. Or, if you put it in your shoes, it would keep the spirits from entering your body through your feet.

Gullahs believe that people have a soul that goes to heaven if they were good and have a spirit that stays behind. If the spirit was a good spirit, it helped the person and his family. If the spirit was a bad spirit, it is known as a boo hog who uses its witchcraft on people. There are ways to keep the boo hog away, but since it is repelled by indigo blue, Gullahs paint the trim, shutters, and ceilings of their houses "haint blue" to keep the boo hogs and spooks out. This custom was carried over even in Charleston, where you can see porch ceilings painted "haint blue."

Many Gullahs still practice some of the customs and juju left from the early slaves. Today, people drive to the villages and hear the residents speak in the wonderful Gullah dialect that was passed down from generation to generation. Some of it has passed into urban culture.

When we traveled, as on those trips past Gullah country, my father usually did most of the driving, even though Mother was a good driver. Before her accident, she would have put my sister and me in the car and driven us to Charleston by herself. But after she hit and killed the colored girl with her car, she wouldn't drive that stretch of road. Instead, she would take the Greyhound bus.

One day during this time, it was just turning dark, and after a day of shopping in Charleston, Mother and I boarded the bus for the trip home from Charleston. We seated ourselves on the first seat by the door, and I started to fall asleep. I sat up when the bus suddenly slowed down and pulled off to the side of the road. I heard people in the back gasping and shouting to the driver, "What happened?" and "Oh, no!" When I looked toward the driver's chair, I saw the lights were off on the speedometer and the other colored dials. Then I saw that the headlights were off, also. Some sort of bus power failure. The driver kept tapping the dashboard, hoping that would make the lights come back on. He looked at my mother and said, "We're just a few miles from Georgetown, so I think we can make it if we drive slowly and can have light held up for us as we go."

He pointed to a handle that was connected to a spotlight on the side of the bus and asked my mother if she would shine it on the edge of the road as he drove. Mother stood next to the door and guided the light on the asphalt and grass that was next to it. I don't think we went any faster than five miles an hour, but we got home. I thought my mother was a hero, and no boo hogs got us.

Another time when we were coming back from shopping, we got to the bus depot later than usual. There were so many white people already in line when we got there that we knew we weren't going to get a good seat. A sign that said "No food or pets allowed on the bus" was posted next to the bus, so people were throwing soda bottles and leftover food in the trash can before the driver checked. My mother handed the tickets to the driver and led me down the aisle. The bus was packed, and the only available seats she could find were in the last row in the white section.

The colored people weren't allowed to sit across from whites, and I watched them walk past us to the colored section. They carried suitcases, boxes, and all kinds of bundles wrapped in pillowcases. The back of the bus was more crowded than our white section. People sat three in a row back there, with children sitting in parents' laps and some even hunkering down on the floor in the aisle. Since buses weren't air conditioned in those days, it was hot, and the odor of so many people was almost unbearable.

As we pulled out of the terminal, I heard people whispering to each other, children laughing, and a baby crying. I tucked my feet up on the seat and fell asleep. It didn't seem like I slept very long until Mother shook me and told me we were home. I put my feet on the floor, expecting to stand up, but pulled them back on the seat when I stepped in a wet stream that was rolling under the seats from the back of the bus. I looked at Mother and asked what it was. She said, "It must have rained during the night and it came in the window." But there wasn't one drop of rain on the windshield and windows, so I didn't know why she said that. I concluded someone in the back must have peed on the floor and Mother was too embarrassed or didn't want to think that we had stepped into pee.

US Highway 17 had been maintained and improved during World War II, when it was used by the military bases in Charleston and Myrtle Beach. All kinds of businesses were scattered now out in the country along the highway. There were a few gas stations, little stores where you could buy milk or bread, and lots of stores to buy fishing supplies and equipment. Another business was the Sunset Lodge, one of the most famous houses of ill repute in the southeast. The "lodge" was near Georgetown's airport on US 17, the Old Charleston Highway. Rumors said the proprietor was connected to the mob, professional baseball, and politicians. I never knew about this and wonder how many people in Georgetown did know about this at the time.

The Georgetown drive-in theatre was about fifteen minutes from my house on Old Charleston Highway. The entrance led to a long dirt drive-way lined with a metal fence that was topped with barbed wire. Drivers stopped at the little shack at the end of the driveway and paid for the tickets. Underneath the sign that said TICKETS, another sign was posted, NO COLORED PEOPLE ALLOWED. Everyone knew the law would not allow colored people to sit in the white section in regular movie houses, and they also knew this law carried over to drive-ins. However, colored people made their own black section in this drive-in by simply sitting outside the metal fence along the driveway.

One Friday night when my father was working the late shift at the paper mill, my mother reluctantly drove my sister, Aunt Christine, and me to see the movie *Frankenstein* with Boris Karloff. The drive-in, located out in the boonies, was frightening enough without watching this scary movie. Aunt Christine was eager to go and sat in the front seat by Mother. My sister and I sat in total fear in the back seat and watched the entire black-and-white movie, with Frankenstein lurching about amidst ominous dark shadows. I was so relieved when it was over.

After the movie ended, my mother drove the car down the long drive-way toward the exit sign. The line was long, and the wait seemed longer. We watched the colored people darting in and out of the trees and bushes along the fence, hoping the drive-in owners wouldn't catch them. Aunt Christine was always a prankster and decided to give these colored people another scare. She rolled down her widow and yelled, "Frankenstein! Frankenstein is gonna get you!" She laughed when the colored people turned and ran back into the trees. I wondered if these colored people were really scared the huge monster was going to get them, or if they were scared a group of whites was going to beat them up.

Every time I watch the old Frankenstein movie, I think about that time at the drive-in and how frightened those colored people must been that night and each day when they were alone in white communities. Their beds weren't made of Dixie's soft goose feathers but were usually pallets made of Spanish moss and leaves shoved into burlap ticking, or with straw and corncobs.

And in a larger sense, both day and night, as at the drive-in, they lurked and walked and slept isolated, outside.

BASEBALL

After the emancipation was declared and the Civil War was over, many Northerners bought the bankrupt plantations of the Southern planters and employed the freed people to continue their work on the sites where they had been slaves. The colored residents worked hard, but in their leisure time they loved to play sports, especially baseball. This sport was said to have been first played by Abner Doubleday before the Civil War, but this myth has been discounted. Baseball evolved out of English and American games with balls and sticks played as long as America has been settled. By the turn of the century, baseball was everywhere, on school grounds, on vacant lots, in parks, and in backyards. It was a sport all Americans enjoyed, whether you were an amateur or professional player or one who enjoyed the thrill of the words the announcer shouted at the start of the game: "Play ball!"

As years passed, in the early twentieth century, the plantation workers from several land holdings in our Charleston area had formed teams, usually playing on Saturdays. The teams required only nine players; entire communities came out to cheer the teams on during the games after World War II. There were several colored sandlot teams when I was a child in Georgetown, composed mostly of black workers. However, when they had a game at Arcadia or Betts Village Plantations, it was known they would ask a few white men to join them.

My father got caught up in the baseball mania of our area. We were a mill culture, and his life centered on the paper mill where he worked. By the start of the twentieth century, baseball teams from mill villages in the South were also thriving alongside the colored teams. During the next half-century, mill-sponsored teams played weekly and had thousands of fans. Sometimes the games were hotly contested, and fights broke out in the stadium and continued outside. If an unpopular call was made, the fans would often storm the field and carry the umpire off.

It isn't a surprise that all of these mill-sponsored teams were white. Even though Jackie Robinson integrated professional baseball in 1947, baseball in South Carolina and in other parts of the country continued segregated. Hardly noticed, in our same area amateur colored teams were also continuing to grow. Integration in the youth leagues came about, slowly.

Getting ahead of my story in the interest of baseball history in the area, I'll say that though we moved away from Georgetown in 1952, my father followed the teams in South Carolina. In 1955, Charleston formed an all-colored team called the Cannon Street All-Stars and entered the state tournament, which was for whites only. Sixty-one white teams, including the team in Georgetown, quit the league rather than play a colored team. They formed an all-white league called Dixie Youth Baseball. That year the colored team from Charleston was declared the state winner due to default when the white team quit. Even so, the team could not participate in the Little League World Series because it had not played in a tournament. However, the Cannon Street All-Stars got an all-expenses-paid trip to Pennsylvania to watch the integrated team from New Jersey play in the Little League tournament. They stayed with the other teams and sat with them during the tournament. When the Cannon Street team and their coaches were introduced before the game, shouts were heard in the bleachers, "Let them play! Let them play!"

The team got on the bus to return to Charleston the next day, August 28, 1955—the same day Emmett Till, a colored boy, was brutally murdered in Mississippi for allegedly whistling at a white woman.

There were so many Jim Crow laws that applied to sports in those days. How outlandish they sound today. In Georgia, one law said, "It shall be unlawful for any amateur white baseball team to play baseball on any vacant lot or baseball diamond within two blocks of a playground devoted to the negro race and it shall be unlawful for any amateur colored baseball team to play baseball in any vacant lot or baseball diamond within two blocks of a playground devoted to the white race." Segregation continued to affect the way games could be played.

I had grown up with all this baseball mania. During the late 1940s and 1950s, baseball was one of the main attractions in Georgetown for us young people. Sandlot games played by teenagers and young boys could be found in almost any vacant lot in town. After school, boys would flock out of the schoolhouse, run home, then head to their games. Some girls followed the boys and cheered on the sidelines when their favorite team scored, but few girls were allowed to join teams on the field.

Although my father loved baseball, he didn't play on one of the mill teams because he was too busy with work and family. He knew the names of the teams and their players, though, and could quote the statistics of these teams. At nights he would sit in his big brown chair and tune into games on our big radio that were broadcast from all over the country. I didn't know any players or team names, but I heard announcers broadcasting from New York, Chicago, and St. Louis. One night I heard someone on the radio talking over and over again about Jackie Robinson. When I asked my father who was Jackie Robinson, the only thing he said was, "He's a good baseball player."

Georgetown had a semi-professional baseball team, the Athletics, which was part of the Palmetto League. Its home games were played in the Georgetown County Stadium, built in the early 1900s. The stadium was still segregated, so the colored teams had to play in fields out in the country. In the 1950s, the paper mill refurbished the Athletics' stadium. The tin wall that surrounded the field was replaced by a concrete one, and a huge scoreboard was installed in left field. These improvements enticed more people to go to the local games. The Athletics played 5 games each week and between 35 and 40 games each season. The stands were packed with about 2,500 spectators at each game. You could feel the excitement in Georgetown when the Athletics were scheduled to play.

I don't think my father missed one home game unless he was working that particular night. Sometimes he would take me to a game. We would have an early supper, then I would pull on an old shirt and pants. I sat on the front seat of the car and watched as he shifted the old Ford through the gears and drove downtown to the park. I would spot the bright lights that perched in the sky over the field and hear the pop of balls being hit by the players as they warmed up.

The crowd was different from the sedate and mannerly crowd at church, no matter which denomination. People at the park seemed to be louder and in a bigger rush to get inside. It only cost 25 cents for children and 35 cents for adults, and Daddy got tickets and led me up the steps to the top section of the stadium. Even though these were the cheap seats, the bleachers were all concrete and had a roof over them. I didn't care where I sat, just so I could see. My mother would complain if we got our clothes dirty, so Daddy carried a newspaper and put it down on the bleacher seats. Someone would start singing "Take Me Out to the Ball Game," the unofficial national anthem of baseball, and I would chime in, shouting, "One, two, three strikes..."

As we shared a bag of peanuts and watched the game, Daddy explained what was happening. That night, the score was close and all of the peanuts were gone, so I nervously ripped up the newspaper into tiny shreds and dropped them onto the concrete floor. At the end of the game my father looked at the floor and laughingly said, "We won't tell your mother what a mess you made."

Going to baseball games with my dad was always thrilling, with a kind of excitement I hadn't known. Whenever one of our players hit the ball and knocked it over the wall, everyone stood and screamed. Children jumped up and down, and the men even hugged each other. Those long, hot summer nights I learned how baseball was played.

Another time Daddy surprised me when he came home from work and asked if I wanted to go to a ball game. It was late and the game probably had already started, but at least we could see some of it. He drove a little faster than usual, and as he turned into the parking lot, we both noticed there weren't many cars there. We went to the ticket booth and found that our Athletics weren't playing; it was an all-colored team that was allowed to use the facility that night. He looked at me and said, "I don't think we should stay." When we got home, my mother wanted to know why we were back so early. He laughed when he said, "It was an all-colored game." That was some kind of a little joke between the two of them, I guess.

I didn't know then (thought my father surely did) that Georgetown had a direct connection to professional baseball. It had to do with our area's well-known South Island Plantation, which became in our time the center for the Yawkey dynasty of the Detroit Tigers. Its history prior to that time had been interesting. South Island was purchased by General Edward Porter Alexander around the close of the nineteenth century. General Alexander had been a commander in the Confederate Army during the Civil War, was a respected engineer, and became one of the most admired chroniclers of the Confederate experience in the war. Georgetown and his plantation drew attention in the newspapers when President Grover Cleveland paid a visit to do some hunting and fishing. The president was tossed out of a hunting skiff into the water when a sudden wind came up. When the news of his rescue was reported in newspapers, people also became aware of the opportunities to hunt and fish on South Island and at the other plantations in South Carolina. But South Island's real future fame was yet to come. My father and all of the men in Georgetown must have known about this connection and relived it whenever they went to the barbershops and hardware stores.

Bill Yawkey, owner of the Detroit Tigers, purchased the South Island Plantation around 1911, then died in 1919. He left his estate and the plantation to his adopted nephew, Tom Yawkey Austin, a real rich-boy character who was also intelligent and perceptive. His legal name became Tom Austin Yawkey.

Tom's adoptive uncle had loved to hunt, attend baseball games, drink, and gamble on horses, and he often brought friends to the plantation for extended stays. He entertained Ty Cobb, Tris Speaker, and other baseball greats. Young Tom Austin Yawkey loved baseball and idolized the players. In 1933, Tom bought the Boston Red Sox and Fenway Park for $1.25 million, a lot of money for a struggling franchise.

He once told Dan Daniel, a writer, "Some men like to spend their dough on fast horses and other things that go fast. Some men like to go in for ponies, for example, and spend thousands of dollars on ponies. Some go nuts over paintings and give half a million for a hunk of canvas in a fancy frame. But my passion is baseball. My idea of heaven is pennant winner. Boston would go nuts over a winner, and maybe someday we'll get all the dough back. But in the meantime, don't let anybody tell you Tom Yawkey is a sucker." Devoted, honest, and crazy for professional baseball. And he was right there in our neighborhood.

Tom's first marriage was failing during the 1930s: Tom's interests were mainly baseball, hunting, and fishing, while his wife's were socializing in New York and Beverly Hills. They separated for a few years, divorced in 1944, and both remarried a few weeks after the divorce. Tom and his second wife, Jean, were married in a private ceremony in Georgetown. They loved the same things: privacy, quiet evenings, and baseball. They became involved in charitable causes in both Boston and Georgetown. In 1950, they donated money to build a new hospital with a nurses' home and laundry building in Georgetown and continued funding other organizations in the county. Later, my father read in one of his newspapers that Yawkey had died in 1976 and willed his 20,000-acre estate to South Carolina's Department of Natural Resources. It consisted of two islands and was to be maintained as a wildlife preserve, a reserve and nature center for the study of migratory birds, eagles, alligators, and many endangered species.

Sportswriter Red Smith once wrote about Tom Yawkey, "He had little in common with other club owners and they were mystified by him, if not suspicious, because he was a strange fish who was in baseball not to make a buck or to feed his ego but because he happened to love the game."

The Yawkey estate, scene of so many of these glamorous events and sporting history, was five miles from our home. I had a girlfriend in elementary school who lived on the reserve, though, and so I got to see it. Her father must have been one of the caretakers who lived there year round. I went home with her after school one day. We rode the yellow school bus to the end of the road and got out. All I could see was the river, a flat wooden raft on the other side and a steel cable hooked on each side of the river. I didn't know how we were going to get across, but my girlfriend crossed this river every day, so I didn't worry. Finally, I saw a colored man coming across the river on the raft. He was pulling the steel cable with some type of wooden pole and maneuvered it to the pier where we were standing. By this time, the colored man was sweating. He wiped his hands on his shirt, lowered his eyes, and said, "Eve'nin Misus," to my friend.

He held the raft steady as we got on, then pulled us across the river, where my friend's mother picked us up. She drove us down a dirt road that went weaving through moss-covered trees and wild bushes with purple berries on them. The two-story house that sat back in the trees was one of the most beautiful homes I had ever seen, let alone been in. My friend and I played in the carpeted living room until dark, ate supper in the kitchen with her mother and father, then went upstairs to her room. The next morning after breakfast, her father took us back to the river where the colored man was waiting on the raft. He pulled us across the river, where we waited for the yellow bus to pick us up and drive us to school.

Why did I never know about this place? I always heard that only colored people lived at the end of the road and it was never safe for whites. And here was this mansion with tons of history and connections to famous people and sports. What other tales were there about secluded places in my hometown? Did my parents know about this island? After all, we lived on South Island Road. That was only about twenty minutes to the ferry that took my friend and me across the river.

When I was an adult, I read that after Tom Yawkey and his second wife married, they didn't want to live in that extravagant house, so he built a house farther in the woods that was less conspicuous. The big house was left for the caretakers and their families. I wonder if that house where my friend lived had originally been the extravagant house Tom built for his first wife.

CHURCH AND PHILANTHROPY

Georgetown has had a history of religious freedom. Temple Beth Elohim has one of the oldest Jewish communities in South Carolina. The graves in its 1722 cemetery are turned to the east, facing Jerusalem. The Duncan Memorial United Methodist Church was established in 1785, making it one of the oldest Methodist churches in the United States. The Antipedo Baptist Church was established in 1750 and St. Mary's Catholic Church in 1899.

Prince George Winyah Episcopal Church has a very interesting history. The second church of that name, the masonry church, was built in 1750 with old bricks from British ships' ballast and oyster shell mortar called tabby. The British held the building during the Revolutionary War, and the Union soldiers held it during the Civil War. The interior of the building was burned when the British left. Legend says that soldiers' horses were stalled in the church's box pews during both wars, and you could see hoofprints of some of the horses underneath the carpet.

Before emancipation, slaves accompanied their owners to church. Most of the time they waited outside, but sometimes they were allowed to stand inside in the back of the church and listen to the ministers. After they were freed, they incorporated many of the practices of the white churches into their own colored Christian churches.

The Bethel African Methodist Episcopal Church was the first separate black church in Georgetown County that was not a part of a plantation. It was established by Reverend Augustus Carr, who was born a slave but later purchased freedom for himself. Before the Civil War, Carr ran a horse livery station in Georgetown. During that war, Southern soldiers would go into the stable with their horses and demand Carr feed their horses without pay. If he asked for pay, sometimes the soldiers would draw pistols and threaten him. It has been estimated that nearly 3,000 freed slaves were members of the church directly after the war, when Reverend Carr became its first minister. This church became the hub of the post-Civil War colored community.

When I was a small child, our family were not "everyday" churchgoing people. The very first church I remember going to was a small Lutheran church in Georgetown that we passed each time we went to town. I had never noticed it before even though the school bus passed it each morning and afternoon. I don't know where my sister or father were, but one Sunday morning my mother decided to go to church. She dressed up in her good brown suit, then pulled my best dress over my head and checked my white orthopedic shoes that were supposed to help my flat feet.

The drive to the church took only a few minutes, but I sat up straight on the front seat, hoping my starched dress wouldn't get wrinkled. It was a hot spring day, but my mother had the windows rolled up so the wind wouldn't blow her hair and dust wouldn't get on us. The small Lutheran wooden church was painted white and had big double doors with metal handles on the front. Its tall steeple had a bell in it, and I could hear it ringing when we got out of the car. Just as we slid into one of the pews, organ music began to play and little boys in white robes walked down the aisle carrying tall white candelabra topped with lit candles. They continued to the front of the church, lit some candles that were on a platform, and then sat down on the first pew. The boys were about my age, and I wondered if any of them were in my second-grade class at school.

It was all new to me. We sang songs and read some pages out of a book, then listened to a man in a white robe talk. I sat quietly through the entire service and wondered why we had to sit and stand so many times. When we got home, I asked my mother, "Why were those boys carrying candles?" She said, "I don't understand it either."

We never went back to that church, but somehow my parents found our way to the First Baptist Church downtown. There wasn't as much sitting down and standing up as we did at that first church, but the preacher's talk was much longer. Sometimes the talks were so boring that I stopped listening to him and would look around at the stained-glass windows and make up stories about angels floating around in heaven. That minister talked a lot about lightning bolts and fire from heaven, and I told my sister, "That scared the liver out of me." Once I fell asleep and my mother scolded me, "You are too old to fall asleep during the sermon. The preacher was looking right at you." But try as hard as I could, my eyelids shut down and I drifted away from all that boring talk.

What I found fascinating about church was what they called communion. I was a little newcomer to religious observation, and so it was foreign and different. On certain Sundays, plates with crackers were passed down the aisle, followed by gold bowls that contained tiny cups with juice. The preacher said that this was somebody's flesh and blood. My mother said I was too young to eat and drink this, but I thought that even if I were old enough I wouldn't want to eat somebody's skin and drink their blood. I asked her about it, and she said, "It's not really blood but just grape juice that turns into blood after you drink it." "Blood! That settles it!" I told myself. "I'll never drink that stuff out of those tiny cups even if it's only grape juice."

My mother, father, and sister were baptized in that church, but later left to be a part of a group establishing a new Baptist church in Georgetown. I was told one of the members had a falling out with the preacher at the First Baptist Church and wanted to start a mission near us in the country. Daddy would go down the road to the neighbor's house for organizational meetings several times a week. One night after a meeting, he sat down at the kitchen table and told us the Southside Mission, as their group was calling itself, had decided to change its name. He had read about William Screven, the founding father of the earliest Baptist church in the South, and my father suggested the group name the church Screven Baptist Church after him. I could tell he was proud that he was the one responsible for the naming of the church. It was also typical of my dad's interest in things beyond the everyday experience, history especially.

After the charter was made official, an itinerant preacher was hired. I liked him because he didn't scare me with talks about lightning bolts and fires like the other preacher did. He laughed a lot and his talks weren't long or boring. Sunday services were held above a grocery store. The lady who taught Sunday school told us nice stories, then gave us a snack. I looked at the purple juice and asked her if it was blood or grape juice. She smiled and said it was Kool-Aid, so I drank it down.

My Sunday schedule was packed and always the same. I went to Sunday school from 10AM to 11AM, which was followed by church services until noon. After dinner at home, my parents had a short nap, then we all studied Bible class material. Training Union, which was like Sunday school but not as formal, was from 6PM to 7PM. Evening church services were from 7PM to 8PM or longer, depending how lengthy the preacher's talk was. We had prayer meetings on Wednesday nights, and the adults had other church meetings during the week. So there was plenty of church, no shortage of churchgoing, for my family in Georgetown.

Revivals were held twice a year. These meetings rejuvenated all of us and brought in new members. Each night we would go to church at the grocery store and listen to visiting preachers. They came from all over the South and talked about what went on in their communities. We prayed a lot and sang songs like "Revive Us Again" and "Bringing in the Sheaves." What were sheaves anyway?

After the meetings were over, I would take my little black Bible and have the visiting preachers sign their autographs on a blank page. I kept it and look at it still. There was Vener Ahinllard from Eunice, Louisiana, and Reverend Ben Bushyhead from Whittier, North Carolina, who wrote his name in Cherokee underneath his regular name. Then there was Thomas L. Meely from Carucas, Venezuela; C. E. Mumuillian from Spartenburg, South Carolina; and Amelia Rappold from Riverfront Mission in New Orleans, Louisiana. It never dawned on me that not one of these missionaries had black skin. The churches in the South were still segregated and the Bible had nothing to do with that. No commands about that in there.

There were wealthy people beyond the Yawkeys who lived in the area and donated money to the local churches as well as to schools. We didn't see them at our churches usually, as they preferred plantation hunting and fishing of a Sunday, or the "watering" experiences of our South Carolina coastline.

My parents were aware of some of the coastal celebrities. Sometimes you could see them driving around town in their convertibles or new sports cars. Occasionally, they were spotted in one of clothing emporiums or the hardware store. Daddy came home once and told us, "I saw Baruch at the barbershop today." I didn't know who this person was, but I assumed it was someone famous. And it was.

Bernard Baruch had a large presence, an estate nearby which we called the Barony. Its full name was Hobcaw Barony. The son of a Jewish German immigrant who lived in South Carolina, Bernard Baruch became a wealthy investor, philanthropist, and presidential advisor, a national figure. In about 1905, Barnard bought fourteen plantations near Georgetown for a winter hunting resort. This new "plantation" was Hobcaw Barony. At his spacious, spreading Georgian-style home, Baruch entertained many famous guests such as Winston Churchill, Omar Bradley, and Robert Taft. When Franklin D. Roosevelt stayed as a guest for several months at the Barony in the hopes it would improve his health, the visit was kept a secret from residents of Georgetown.

Baruch was generous with his money and donated to black colleges in South Carolina. He made sure there were black beds for patients in previously limited white hospitals and paid for the education of colored children who grew up in the local villages. When he died, the Barony became property of the Belle W. Baruch Foundation. The estate was designated as a nature preserve in the name of daughter Belle, who had gradually taken over management and ownership of the properties.

We benefitted from the philanthropists who seemed to thrive in the area. In 1932, Archer Huntington donated 1,600 acres of land for a public sculpture garden and nature reserve to showcase his wife's sculptures. This became the internationally known Brookgreen Gardens. We loved to go there in the 1940s and take out-of-town relatives for the day. My sister and I would climb on the big marble statues and put our feet in the pools underneath the fountains.

Archer Huntington's father had been a railroad magnet and industrialist who amassed a large fortune in the 1800s. When Archer inherited this fortune, he bought four plantations in the Georgetown area for a winter home and a place for his wife, Ann Hyatt Huntington, to create her sculptures. Two of these plantations were Springfield and Laurel Hill. Another, Brookgreen Plantation, had been the home of Joshua John Ward, who had been the largest slaveholder in America before the Civil War. Ward had owned 1,092 slaves. Prior to Ward's ownership, the plantation was owned by Joseph Alston, whose wife was Theodosia Burr, the daughter of Aaron Burr. Theodosia was lost at sea; her ghost is said to haunt the beaches nearby and the memorial grave in Brookgreen Garden, where my sister and I waited for her to appear. We would stand on the memorial and ask, "Theodosia, what are you are doing down there?" Then we would laugh and say,

"She said, 'Nothing.'"

Archer was a scholar of Spanish culture and art, so he designed their thirty-room mansion in the style of Moorish architecture and called it Atalaya Castle. There were rooms for servants, but the castle had no guest rooms or formal dining room. Ann's sculptures were life size, and he built pens for live animals, including stallions, dogs, bears, wild cats, and monkeys, to serve as her models. When the two of them traveled cross-country, they pulled a special trailer so they could take their dogs, monkeys, and birds. In 1932, he donated money for Holy Cross Faith Memorial Parish House and School for colored and poor children in the area. This was a turning point in this Episcopal church's history.

These were all wealthy white men and women, shaping the philanthropic destinies of the town where I was a child. Were there never black givers? Years later, when I was grown and watching *60 Minutes,* I heard a story about a Pawleys Island area woman of my parents' era that fascinated me. She too benefited the area significantly, where she and her husband had run the nationally famous schools at Holy Cross Faith Memorial.

Ruby Middleton, granddaughter of slaves, was born in Charleston in 1905. Her father was a bricklayer, and her mother ironed the local white nurses' and doctors' uniforms. After Ruby married Reverend Forsyth, a black Episcopal minister, she began teaching in the one-room school next to his church. They lived on the second floor of the school building in Pawleys Island and held classes on the first floor. The school was the only one in the area open to colored children. She started teaching at this school before there were bridges that connected the marshes to the mainland, before electricity, and before integration and civil rights.

She taught in that school for fifty-three years, and it became known as "Miss Ruby's School." She said, "I teach all the basics plus the little things that count: honesty, dependability, and responsibility." During the early days of her tenure at the school, the white community wanted colored children to stay in their places and not achieve outside of their local boundaries. Miss Ruby taught the children to understand they were a part of the whole world.

Miss Ruby had been written about in *Life Magazine,* was on Johnny Carson's *Tonight* Show, as well as *60 Minutes.* I wondered, "Why hadn't I known about this marvelous woman when I was a little girl?"

In the 1990s, my sister and I decided to go on a pilgrimage to George-town. For some reason, I was compelled to see the Miss Ruby, whose educational leadership with black children had intrigued me. We stopped at several gas stations and restaurants and asked for directions to her home.

No one seemed to know who she was until one colored man said, "Oh, the black lady who has that church out toward Pawleys Island." We followed Highway 17 over the bridge and headed toward Holy Cross School. As we turned into the long drive, I saw a car pulling out from the back of the church. There was a tiny black woman behind the wheel. For some reason I knew that was Miss Ruby, so I jumped out of the car and rushed to her. I don't remember what I mumbled to her, but her face lit up and she invited us into her school. Maybe it was because I told her I was from Arizona and had come to meet her, or maybe it was because my sister and I had lived in Georgetown and wanted to know about her.

We stayed for a while, fascinated, as she told us about her students and the school. She told us that Archer Huntington had given money for the school. She also talked about Belle Baruch, who would come into a room after she had been riding horses all day and put her dirty boots up on the table. As we sat around a table, she began talking about Hurricane Hugo that had come through South Carolina in 1989. The island and area had been evacuated, but she decided to stay. She sat back and told us, "I stayed downstairs in the school room. About midnight the trees started falling and shingles on the roof began blowing off. Even the old chimney groaned as the wind picked up." I listened in awe to this remarkable story, then said, "Oh, Miss Ruby, you must have been so afraid, and you were so alone." She took my hand in her old black one, stared into my eyes, and said, "Honey, I wasn't alone. My Lord was with me."

This same kind of hope and deep faith must have helped sustain many of the colored people who were enslaved on these plantations. After the Civil War, freed slaves and their descendants rose to useful and prominent places in our United States history, and many of them, like Miss Ruby, cultivated and broadcast love and kindness.

A sign hanging over the door of her school says, "Miss Ruby's philosophy: Never say I can't. Always say I can."

Little Lou Ellen with big sister Margaret. We have stayed close all our lives and took a sentimental trip back to the Georgetown area to see the old sights in the 1990's.

My parents helped organize a new Baptist chruch in Georgetown. First called Southside Mission of the First Baptist Church, my dad suggested it be called Sceven Baptist Church after the first Baptist minister to serve the South. My dad Bernie Overhultz is 6th from the left, top row; mother Dollie first woman seated; and I am first row kneeling. 1950.

Our old brown Ford. This is the car we drove to see the house where a cross had been burned.

I'm with my best friend Kathleen Lee. There was so much to do in our sandy neighborhood in South Carolina, roaming with friends, dressing up, or investigating mysterious, overgrown lots.

My Dad worked at this Georgetown paper mill for fifteen years. It opened in 1937 and now, as International Paper, has 600 employees.

Father Bernie Overhultz and daughter Lou Ellen, perhaps at the Middleton Gardens. He loved exploring.

Mom and Dad, shown here in the 1940s, met
at the paper mill in Arkansas and were married
in 1932. He spent his entire life as a paper
processor.

My aunt Christine Roberts was a modern gal, always seeking excite-
ment. Her hussband Garland worked at the paper mill too.

Typical raised houses on the road to Pawleys Island, taken on our return trip in the 1990s. Our quiet and rather remote vacation spot in the 1940s has become a mecca for tourists and the site of beautiful homes: an American destination.

Mary Scott is the "Gullah Weaver" along the road today. We often drove by the Gulluah settlement as children, viewing it as a mysterious and ominous spot because of its remoteness and the rumors of Voodoo practices.

The old slave market in Charleston. I shuddered each time we walked through it. It turns out it never actually sold slaves.
(r) Mary practiced writing her name so she could autograph my book

Bernard Baruch's Hobcow Barony estate home. Belle Baruch, his daughter (insert, Belle Baruch Foundation photo) was a philanthropic contributor to the Charleston area and a bit of a character.

Miss Ruby Forsythe and her husband established a school at Holy Cross Faith Memorial Church, where he was the minister. It was the only school in the area for black children for some years. My sister and I visited her on our trip back to Georgetown.

Baseball legend Tom Yawkey had an estate near us. Perhaps I was inside his house once, visiting a friend.

MOBILE ALABAMA 1952-1955

MOBILE: OLD SHELL ROAD

I was about to start seventh grade, 1952. The Korean War was going on. Dwight D. Eisenhower had been elected president; Queen Elizabeth II was the new queen of England. We watched *I Love Lucy*, *I've Got a Secret*, and *The Today Show* on TV and heard about Kentucky Fried Chicken's first franchise opening in Salt Lake City.

Civil rights issues began to be on the news, too. Segregation and Jim Crow politics still dominated the South. Black people didn't attend our schools, eat at our restaurants, swim in our pools, or even enter many public places, but rumblings of change were starting to be felt across the land. *The Chicago Tribune* and the NAACP reported that 1952 was the first time in seventy years there were no reports of lynchings. Even so, acts of violence against blacks, such as executions, bombs, arsons, and beatings, seemed to be increasing.

International Paper Company was transferring my father to Mobile, Alabama, giving him a promotion and a substantial raise in salary. My parents had lived in Georgetown for seventeen years, since the paper mill first opened, and my sister had started first grade and graduated from high school there. I had finished sixth grade and was now leaving friends that I had known for twelve years. I had to say goodbye to Angela, Joyce, Kathleen, and my next door boyfriend Johnny.

We were on a limited moving budget and had to be selective in what we took. My mother began the task of sorting things out and packing. Some of my favorite dolls and teddy bears had to be given away, as well as my sister's collections of records and movie star posters. Finally, the dreaded day came, and my mother, sister, and I got in the car and headed out. As we pulled out of the driveway, my mother started crying. I didn't realize at the time how traumatic it must have been for her. Moving meant she was leaving behind memories and her friends.

That summer of 1952, as we pulled into the city limits of Mobile, I looked out the side window of the car and gawked at the sign, "WELCOME TO MOBILE – elevation 9.843 feet – population 130,000 and growing." I had read a little about the city before we left and found out Mobile had known real action and devastation during the Civil War. Afterwards, it had risen again with the production of steel and shipbuilding during World War I and World War II. This rebuilt city had been known by many nicknames, such as the Port City, the Big Oyster, the Azalea City, and the City of Perpetual Promises, but really could have been called the City of Southern Graciousness.

Following my dad's leaning towards history and learning, I was interested in the town's background. Historians still write about the Battle of Mobile Bay in 1864. The Union had eighteen ships in the bay, which included four ironclad monitors. Its commander, Rear Admiral David G. Farragut, ordered his fleet to ignore the Confederate defenses and shouted his famous proclamation, "Damn the torpedoes, full speed ahead!" The Confederate troops were outnumbered and surrendered.

Archaeological excavations were trying to find the *Clotilda*, the last known ship that brought 110 slaves from Africa to the United States in 1860. The captain of this two-masted schooner, afraid his illegal slave trade would become known, had the ship scuttled in Mobile Bay. The slaves were dispersed to plantation owners and others in the area. After the Civil War, some of these slaves made their way back to the bay and founded a community called Africatown. The last known survivor of the original group died in 1935. So their history went.

My father stayed at the Battle House Hotel in Mobile until he found us a house on Old Shell Road. It was a two-bedroom brick house with a screened porch and large backyard. When my mother saw the house, she said, "It'll do for now. It's near the school and the bus line to downtown." She missed her friends already and remembered her quaint little house in the country in Georgetown.

Old Shell Road Junior High was right across the street from our house, so that made it easy for me to get to school. It was a typical two-story brick building with high ceilings, transoms over each door, and wooden floors that were mopped daily with some kind of smelly oil. It was hard making friends, but many students were new also to junior high and seemed to have the same problems as I did. We all nervously looked around and gradually got to know each other.

The smartest student in the seventh grade was a boy who told us the latest news each morning as we waited outside for the bell to ring. We never asked where he got this news. It was probably newspapers or radio but could have been on television, even though news on TV was limited. David always told us fascinating new things. He announced one day, "There's a new card out now that you can use to buy things with and you don't have to use money." We were amazed and asked, "How would you do that? How is it done?" He explained, "You just show the card and they put the amount of the item you are buying on a piece of paper." He continued, "People can use this card all over the world." How wonderful. Could it be true? David was so smart that we never questioned him.

One morning while we were in the schoolyard waiting for the bell to ring, David announced that Stalin was dead. We all knew about Joseph Stalin and Russia, so we all jumped up and down and cheered. Then he turned and said in a serious tone, "We shouldn't be so happy because we don't know who will take his place." Even though we were happy the fierce leader was dead, we were only twelve years old and had never thought about the next step in this situation. He looked at us and stated in a matter-of-fact voice, "There might be somebody worse."

David kept us abreast of the world, but we never knew what was happening under our own noses in Alabama.

Each December, Old Shell Road Junior High was involved in its traditional Christmas program. There were several choirs, speaking narrations, and what they called "living pictures." The teacher selected different scenes of Yuletide living: Santa Claus coming to town, snow falling, and the opening of Christmas presents. Students in costumes lined up behind a wooden 10 x 12 foot frame and stood frozen while the choirs sang songs about each picture. All of us hoped we would be selected to be in one of the pictures.

Finally, the teacher announced the parts for that year's play. I was to be in the pictures portraying choirs singing carols. I overheard the teacher say, "We selected these students because they are the brightest and will be able to follow directions." And they chose me! This made me so proud since I was to be standing next to David, that seventh-grade news reporter, the smartest kid in the class.

If David was the smartest boy in the seventh grade, Billy was the best looking and the best athlete. All the girls wanted to sit by him in class, and everyone wanted Billy to be on his or her team when we chose sides for games. This was the time when we wore black and white saddle shoes and penny loafers with white bobby socks. Our circle skirts were made from yards of material and swished around our legs when we walked. We wore cotton blouses and made sure the little nylon colored scarves that we tied around our necks matched the color of our skirts. Sometimes on special occasions we wore full taffeta dresses with matching belts. I was never really aware of what the boys wore, but I did notice Billy wore corduroy pants and cotton shirts. Mobile's climate was mild, so we never had to worry about snow boots, but we did have to worry about ruining our shoes during the city's seemingly constant rain.

Social studies was the worst class for all of us. Each day the teacher had students stand up and read several paragraphs out of the textbook. She would start at the first row, point to the person, and read along with the student. This continued as each person took a turn. Some were good readers, but most had trouble pronouncing all those strange words about, or from, other countries. We all held our breath when it was good-looking Billy's turn to read. He was a profound stutterer. The teacher told him several times to stand up and read. Reluctantly, he slid out of his desk and began the agonizing process of trying to get all of the words out. I kept my eyes down on the book and wanted to cover my ears. The stammering continued until the bell rang and we all rushed out. We all knew that this was something that shouldn't have happened to one of our classmates. Most of us had learned to be kind to each other. We knew the rules of fairness, and just as we practiced it in our games at recess, wanted to see it in our teachers. No one really said anything to Billy, but we all were embarrassed for him and angry at the teacher for making him read aloud.

I was continuing my interest in music. Back in Georgetown and since I was five years old, I had been taking piano lessons from Mrs. Stokes. She was a large, loving lady who sat next to me on the piano bench each week at my lesson and guided my hands over the keyboard. Each day after school I had to practice for thirty minutes on the upright carved mahogany piano that my sister had started her lessons on, too. This daily agony of pounding at scales and trying to improve my precision seemed like an eternity, since I would rather be outside running and playing. My mother put a wooden switch on top of the piano, which served as a threat of what would happen if I didn't practice. Later, she gave in a little and told me I could practice for fifteen minutes, then go play outside, then come back in and practice fifteen minutes more. She set the alarm on a clock for fifteen minutes and put it put on top of the piano. I would start practicing as she walked out of the room, but after about five minutes, I would set the dial on the clock ten minutes ahead then sneak out the front door to freedom. I don't know if my mother ever caught on to this scheme, but it seemed to work for me.

When I was in fourth grade, I won a piano contest, and my beloved piano teacher, Mrs. Stokes, told my mother I had progressed so much that I should take lessons from the advanced teacher in the town. This teacher was fierce, or at least she seemed to be to a third-grader like me. She would mark the music up with a red pencil at places where I needed to practice more, sometimes even making holes in the music. If my fingernails were too long, she would pull out long, sharp nail clippers and snap the nails shorter. I was always scared she would cut my fingers off. The worst torture of the lessons was when she would take a ruler and hit my knuckles when I made a mistake. The ruler would come down with a smack, then she would yell and point to the note on the music that I missed. I was the youngest of her students, and I don't think she knew anything about young children and their capacities. That was music in Georgetown.

When we got settled in Mobile, my mother wanted me to continue piano, so she started searching for a new teacher. She found one who had a studio in an old two-story brick building near downtown. She dropped me off at the front of the building and pointed to the entrance. I walked up the musty-smelling dark stairs and knocked on the door that had the teacher's name. It opened, and behind a wall of hanging plastic beads a voice welcomed me in. I had never seen a hanging bead wall before, so I stood there wondering what to do. The teacher swept the beads to one side and motioned me in. She was very friendly and showed me around the studio, then picked up an accordion from a table. Carefully, she strapped the instrument to herself and began squeezing it in and out while playing the keyboard. It sounded OK to me, but I had never heard an accordion before, much less seen one. Finally, she put the accordion back on the table and guided me to the upright piano. Before I sat down, she struck a match and lit some incense that was in a little boat-like container on top of the piano. The smoke swirled around to the top of the ceiling and eventually made its way to me. I thought the smoke smelled like something out of the jungle, and even though I began to cough, she didn't seem to notice. At last the thirty-minute lesson was over, and I couldn't wait to get out of there and get some fresh air. The jingling wall of beads slapped my face as I pushed them apart. As soon as I found the door, I pushed it open and ran down the stairs, not even saying goodbye to the teacher. I had read about gypsies that had hanging beads, incense, and accordions. Was she one?

My mother realized this was not the teacher she had in mind, so she found another teacher who taught only piano. No accordions were in sight in his lodgings. He had a degree in piano and had performed all around the country before he retired. However, he slept on a cot through most of my lessons.

Somehow, my mother found Dawn Petersen's Charm School of Dance on Government Street, which was advertised as "MOBILE'S FORE-MOST DANCING STUDIO with air conditioned studios." It offered classes in tap, ballet, baton twirling, acrobatics, voice, and modeling. This sounded like fun to me, so each Saturday my mother paid $2.00 and I had lessons on how to sing in front of an audience.

TV stations were starting to open all over the country. In January 1953, the WALA television station was signing on in Mobile for its first program and invited the charm school students to perform. The director of the school selected two other girls and me to sing, "Stars Fell On Alabama." My mother and I arrived early that morning and entered the back stage door. Dancers were in one corner backstage, baton twirlers in another, and acrobatics were scattered all over. It was bedlam. I found the other members of my trio, and we stuck together wondering what to do. The director spotted us and took us to the TV cameras, where we were to get a run-through before the performance. He showed us the big, unfamiliar giant of a silver camera on rolling wheels and told us to look directly at the little round tube when we sang. He emphasized that when the red light on the camera came on, we were being televised. We needed to stand still until the light went out.

The "Stars Fell On Alabama" girls performed and were the hit of the show. Our director kept getting requests for us to perform for other events, but I had to bid that all goodbye again when my family moved to another state. That was the start of another chapter in my life, but it is ahead of our story.

MARDI GRAS AND SHOPPING

When my parents and I had moved to Mobile from South Carolina, we had begun the task of adjusting to the city. I loved it when my parents took us on what I called "our Sunday drive" to interesting places. We saw the Oakleigh House that was built in 1833 on thirty-five acres. Its third owner defended it during the Civil War from Union soldiers by telling them she was a British citizen. She then hung the British Union Jack flag over the balcony. The Bragg-Mitchell Mansion was built in 1855 and withstood some of the devastation of the Civil War. All of the live oak trees were cut down so the Confederate soldiers could get an unobstructed view of any Union soldiers approaching.

My favorite place to visit was Bellingrath Gardens and Home. In the middle of the seventeenth century, a resident of Mobile planted azaleas he had obtained from France. The plants thrived and became more and more popular with the passing of time. In 1917, Walter Bellingrath, a Coca-Cola executive, and his wife bought a fishing camp on one of the rivers. The couple began planting azaleas, camellias, and other flowering plants. They fell in love with the area and built their fifteen-room house to blend in with the foliage. Later, they opened the house and lavish gardens to the public.

In 1929, citizens lined the street with azalea plants and painted a pink line down the middle of the street. This was the beginning of the traditional Azalea Trail. The Azalea Trail festival brings thousands of tourists into the city to visit the antebellum homes and gardens. Many of the azalea bushes that were planted years ago have become as tall as twenty-foot trees. In early years, Miss America was always part of the parade that opened the festival. She would ride in an open-topped convertible while her trail maids, dressed in pastel Civil War-era hooped skirts, followed with flowery parasols. The Trail Maid Court became so popular in the 1950s that these girls came from all over the southeast, bidding to become one of this festival's southern belles.

Mardi Gras is one of the biggest celebrations in the area. Mobile was the first city to celebrate this event, even predating Mardi Gras in New Orleans.

It was started by a Frenchman in 1703 when Mobile was the capital of Louisiana. Mobile claims that in 1858 members of a Mardi Gras committee traveled to New Orleans and helped set up the first Mardi Gras society in its history. Thousands of Alabamans and out-of-state visitors come to participate in the parades sponsored by various societies in the city. The members of these societies ride on the floats and throw trinkets, beads, and candy to the spectators. Schools and government offices close their doors on certain days of the celebration.

Mobile's downtown was much larger than the one in Georgetown, and traveling from one part of the town to another was a challenge. We had two cars, but my mother didn't like to drive downtown and find a parking place along the street. It was simpler to catch the city bus, which ran just three blocks from our house.

One nice spring day, after we'd been in Mobile for several months, Mother and I got all dressed up to go shopping downtown. We rushed out the back door and made it to the stop just as the bus pulled up. The bus seemed to have more people on it than on other days. Usually, the front of the bus where the white people sat would be almost empty and the back of the bus where the colored people sat would have been filled. That day the white seats were almost filled, but my mother and I were still able to squeeze onto one of the benches next to an old lady.

The bus rambled on down the street but seemed to be making more stops than usual. As we got closer to town, the streets became crowded with people and automobiles. At times the bus driver had to wait for cars that edged in front of the bus from the side streets. He constantly blew his horn at the flow of pedestrians who walked in front of the bus without looking. The bus inched down the street, but soon the driver turned and said, "The next stop will be the closest one to downtown since I have to make a detour because of the parade that's just starting." My mother and I looked at each other and wondered what parade he was talking about. Everyone exited at the next stop and started walking downtown. We were new in town and had forgotten that this was Mardi Gras season! I was excited. We were going to see some of the parades I had heard about.

Downtown was filled with throngs of revelers, and we were in the middle of them. The police department put up barricades so no one could step in the middle of the street and get hit by one of the floats. When the first float appeared, people edged toward the barricades and began shouting and waving, hoping they could catch some candy or beads. My mother grabbed my hand and began pulling me back toward a storefront. When some colored people accidently bumped into us, my mother looked at me and said, "Phew, they stink." I didn't seem to notice.

The parade wasn't over, but my mother pushed me into one of the elegant department stores. The first thing I noticed was the sweet smell of perfume that drifted over the front of the store. Bottles of perfumes in delicate glass containers were displayed on the counters, where women were spritzing themselves with the fragrant samples. Along the aisle I saw all kinds of jewelry for women in the glass cases. Special lights were turned on inside these cases so the rhinestones would sparkle and glimmer. The wooden floors led to the back where a "moving stair" carried women to the second floor and the shoe department. Next to it was a regular stair that was less intimidating. This was pretty impressive to a country girl. I pulled my mother to the "moving stair" and got on. The wooden steps clanked as they reached the top and folded into themselves. I hoped my shoes or socks wouldn't get caught in the cracks. I wondered if my shoes got ripped off and my toes got caught, would the moving stair stop? The ride was loud, jerky, and smelled of grease and oil, but it was fun.

My mother loved shoes, so she looked around at the displays, then found us chairs to wait for service to try the shoes on. A clerk came over immediately and introduced himself, then asked the usual, "What can I do for you today?" My mother pointed to a pair of shoes and asked to see them in her size. While the clerk was in the back searching for the shoes, a well-dressed colored lady walked over from the stairs and looked around. She didn't sit down but leaned against the wall instead. The clerk soon came back with the shoes and helped my mother try them on. They didn't fit, so he took them back to search for a different size. Soon, more ladies came up the "moving stair" and began to look around. They sat down to wait for the clerk.

By the time the clerk came back, all of the chairs were taken by white ladies. The head of the department called for more shoe clerks, who came immediately. One by one, each lady was waited on except the colored lady who was leaning against the wall. Finally, she went to a clerk and asked for a certain shoe. The clerk seemed very nervous, returned with the requested shoe, and said, "You can't try this shoe on in the store. You have to take it home before you try it on." The colored lady said something, which prompted the clerk to say, "Go over in the corner behind the curtain and try it on. Don't let anyone see you."

The clerk must have known it was against most store policies in the South for colored people to try on clothes or shoes on the premises. The colored customers had to buy the item and take it home. If it didn't fit, they weren't allowed to return it. Either way, they would lose. I watched while the colored lady slid the curtain back and leaned against the wall. She put her purse on the floor, pulled off her own shoes, and took the new ones out of the box. Her big feet looked swollen and sore to me, and I saw her strain as she struggled with the new shoes.

All of the white ladies were seated in plush chairs where clerks carefully slipped shoes on and off of their feet. I heard some of the clerks say, "You have the most beautiful feet. Any shoes would look wonderful on your feet." I don't know if the colored lady bought the shoes or if the clerk put them back in the original box and placed it on the shelf. My mother was happy with her new shoes, and when she went to the cash register to pay, the clerk said, "Remember, you can always return them for thirty days." I felt confused at this discrepancy and wondered if all stores in this "big city" were like this.

The Mobile white community seemed to think the Jim Crow laws were quite all right, but many who were suppressed felt the agony of being treated as second class and were beginning to show determination not to tolerate it. I wasn't aware of the demonstrations and violence that were taking place in other parts of the state, but I had heard about the Ku Klux Klan group that was holding cross burnings and recruiting new members, right here in Mobile. I wasn't sure what the organization was all about, but I remembered that cross burning when I lived in Georgetown and knew I wanted to stay away from these scary people in Mobile.

BACK OF THE BUS

It was Mobile, 1953, and still an age of innocence for me. We had moved to Mobile the year before, and I had never heard the actual terms "segregation" or "integration." My world was so sheltered. I was trying to cope with my own problems and my own growing up. True, the shoe incident had provoked my curiosity, but not much else. It would take a startling incident to do that.

The previous year, I had attended the school across from my house, near enough that I could walk. This year, for eighth grade, I had to walk three blocks to catch the city bus that went downtown to my new school, Barton Junior High. I had made friends the year before at Old Shell Road School, and most of them had transferred with me to Barton. I don't know how they got to school, but they didn't ride the city bus with me.

It was a spring day that started off like any other day in eighth grade. I grabbed my books and slipped out the back door of our home, debating whether to cut across the neighbor's yard to save time or take the longer way to the bus stop. The neighbor's new dog was sitting on their back steps, and I wasn't sure if he would attack. I wasn't even sure the neighbors knew who I was. They might come out in their pajamas and yell at me or call the police, so I decided to play it safe and walk the extra block around the corner.

It seemed like it rained all the time in Mobile, but the streets were dry this morning. Even when it wasn't raining, moisture always blanketed the area, and I had to be careful not to slide on the wet moss that covered the sidewalk. My shoes always seemed to be coming untied, and the strings dragged through green slime. Azalea bushes hung over the sidewalk and brushed against me. If I didn't watch out, the waxy branches would leave green splotches on my skirt and blouse. Since no cars came down the side street this early in the morning, the quiet was interrupted only by chirping birds, a few barking dogs, and the sound of people in nearby houses getting ready for the day.

I walked on at a steady pace, clutching my bulky books and papers close to my chest as if they were important military records. If I were a Boy Scout or a military person, then I could have a backpack and could put all of my stuff in

Sleeping in Dixie's Feather Bed

it, but I wasn't even a Girl Scout. I looked around me in appreciation of all I was experiencing in this city on a spring morning. It began drizzling as I stopped on the curb and gazed at all of the large azalea bushes that had just come into bloom. The magnolia trees arched over the street and blocked out the remaining sun. The traffic was never heavy this time in the morning, so I casually crossed the street and stood next to the green metal sign marked BUS STOP. I stuck my hand into my pocket and dug out money for the bus fare. I pulled out the coin and clutched it tightly so I would have it immediately for the coin box on the bus.

In the distance I heard the clunking of the bus and smelled the diesel fumes. It always seemed like the diesel odor reached the stop before the bus did. The green and yellow bus with its white roof was lumbering down the street. With a creak, the door folded open, and the driver in khaki shirt and pants stared at me. His brown hat with its large Alabama logo plastered on the front seemed to declare an official statement. He jerked his head to the side, indicating for me to hurry up. The bus was about a foot away from the curb, which made the first step into the bus hard to reach unless you stepped into the trash-filled gutter. Even though I was a little girl, barely 4'10" tall, I tried to be tough, so I clutched my books close to my chest, made one jump, grabbed the shiny handle, and pulled myself up on the step. The driver seemed to pay no attention, and I quickly deposited the coin in the square metal box, where it clanked against the other coins.

The front of the bus, where the white passengers sat, was almost empty. Quickly, I glanced around and walked to a seat toward the back entrance of the bus where I could look out at oak and magnolia trees lining the street. A yellow line was painted on the floor marking the two seating areas: the white section and the colored section. Before I could sit down, the driver slammed the front door closed and the bus lumbered off.

Sometimes the driver didn't stop for colored people, and sometimes he would go so fast that the bus splashed water on them. When the bus did pull over to pick up passengers, the colored people waited for the white people to get on. After making sure the whites were settled, the driver would nod to the coloreds, who stepped to the front door, leaned over without putting their feet on the step, put their coins in the square tiller, then walked around to the back door. If they didn't get to the back door soon enough, the bus driver would often slam the door, pull away from the curb, and leave the stranded colored passengers on the side of the street, already paid up but abandoned.

As we got closer to downtown, the back of the bus became very crowded. The front remained virtually empty except for a few white passengers who regularly took this commute each day. The colored people greeted each other and stepped closer together to make room whenever more people got on. Some stood and gave their seats to others who needed to sit. I listened as they talked about their families and heard some laughing as they stood side by side. Most of the women had on dark dresses and draped white aprons over their arms. They were ready to take up jobs in the pretty homes with azalea shrubs around the doors. They were The Help. The colored men had old felt hats pulled down on their heads and wore brown pants and shirts. Their lunches were in brown bags that they clutched closely in their callused hands.

At each stop, the driver seemed to be more and more agitated and slammed the brakes more aggressively each time. The creaking of the door became more pronounced when the driver yanked it open and jerked it closed. Perhaps he had personal problems or just was irritated at having to drive for so many "nigras." I would never know. What I did know was that without warning, the bus lurched sideways and stopped so quickly that all of the passengers fell forward. I slid off the seat and dropped my books on the muddy floor. It was so sudden that I couldn't understand what happened and thought it must be a wreck.

The driver got out of his seat and grabbed the silver handle on the door. Pulling with both hands he yanked the door open and jumped out onto the curb. As he ran to the back door I could hear him screaming. He pulled the door open and jumped onto the first step, then began pushing himself past the colored passengers. He stopped at the yellow line on the floor, then yelled, "You niggers will not step past this here line! Do you understand?" I froze, not understanding what was happening. At first I thought someone was hurt and that the ambulance was on the way. I thought, "Maybe I should ask one of the white people what's happening." But as I looked around, all of the few white passengers were just staring straight ahead in silence as if nothing was happening.

One old colored woman had fallen, and some men were trying to help her up. A pregnant lady was moaning and made some protesting remarks. This seemed to make no difference to the driver. He shoved the colored people further back behind the yellow line, really on top of each other, then shouted louder, "YOU will not even put your toe on this here yellow line or I will kick you off this bus! Do you understand?" The colored passengers were pushed together so tightly there was no way they could move. It was as if they were black dominoes standing side by side holding each other up so they wouldn't fall. The air was so thick with the smell of diesel fuel and human bodies that it was amazing no one fainted. I was never consciously aware of overt segregation and the rules regulating this town and the entire south until that precise moment. I only felt sorrow immediately for each of the colored passengers. It didn't seem right.

I looked back to see if the pregnant woman and the old lady who fell down were OK, then in a soft, shaking I voice spoke up, "There's a lot of room here. I'll just move up closer to the front." All the white passengers turned and stared at me as if I had leprosy or was from another planet. The bus driver in his "official" hat stopped his pushing and vulgar language and walked toward me. Through gritted teeth he spouted, "You just sit down right where you are, young lady, and these people will do what I tell them to do." He looked at the bewildered colored faces and stated, rather than asked, "WON'T YOU!" He turned and stomped through the aisle of the bus to his big chair up front. He eased himself down behind the wheel, grabbed the silver handle, pulled the door closed, and started up. No one said a word. There was no more laughter or talk about families. It was a hurtful silence.

As the bus traveled down the street, people would signal the driver to stop by pulling the overhead cord that made a buzzing noise. One by one the white passengers left, leaving only the colored ones to continue to the homes where they cleaned and did yard work. I sat there afraid and confused about what just happened. My stop was coming up next, so I reached up and also pulled the cord, signaling the driver to stop. I took my books and staggered down the aisle to the front of the bus. It seemed like hundreds of eyes followed me, but maybe it was the eyes in back of my own head that followed my distress.

The bus with the diesel fumes continued its path downtown while I watched from the curb. Across the street was my new school Barton Junior High. I knew that it had opened in 1839 for children from several private Christian denominations and now it was public. It had stood there for 113 years, watching as events passed by its door. On the other side of the tall black iron fence that encompassed the school were my classmates, and not one of them was black. This was the beginning of a process of my awakening to what was around me. Things were not going to change soon, though. Though I didn't know it, a seamstress named Rosa Parks was thinking about discrimination in her life in Montgomery, Alabama, and the more she thought about it, the less she liked it. My own discomfort on a segregated bus in Mobile would be a plan for action on a bus in Montgomery for her. But I was blissfully unaware.

"Living Pictures," Old Shell Road Junior High, December 5, 1952. I'm on the right. We weren't really singing, just "frozen" in the pose of singing a carol.

Barton Academy in Mobile was one of the schools I attended. It had a venerable history: its architecture is Greek Revival and after years of construction it opened in 1852 as a public school.

BASTROP, LOUISIANA
1955-1959

HIGH SCHOOL DAYS— IN BASTROP, LOUISIANA

The summer of 1955 arrived. My father came home and told us he had received a promotion and was being transferred again—to Bastrop, Louisiana. My mother must have been upset. She had just hired an interior designer to make curtains for our house. We had been in Mobile for only three years, but I had made friends at school, and my parents were involved in Dauphin Baptist Church activities. It was our life and now it would be shifting again.

My father had already moved to Bastrop, so the driving was left to my mother and sister, who was home from college for the summer. As we drove into the city limits, we saw the paper mill looming in the sky before us with its smoke stacks spewing gray film over the town. The car windows were open and a blast of air swept in. I gagged and shouted, "Roll the windows up! What is that rotten egg smell?" My mother said, "That's the town's bread and butter." I thought, sarcastically, "That doesn't smell like any bread and butter I know." The economy of the town was dependent on the mill.

In this town, as everywhere else still in that day and age, most of the women did their washing on Mondays. My mother would say to me, "Go look outside and see which way the wind is blowing." If the wind was blowing paper mill smog toward our house, she would wait to hang the wash out. The rotten egg smell would dictate a lot of what we did in that town. We would discover some people had window air conditioners and could avoid the smell during the summer, but those without air conditioners, like my family, would just suffer. If the windows were opened on summer nights, I would cover up my face with my pillow so I wouldn't have to take in that offensive stench. But all that was yet to come on this day when we first viewed the town, confronting that stink for the first time.

While my mother drove slowly down the black, sticky asphalt road into the town, I sat on the edge of the back seat looking out at what was to be my new home. The outskirts of town we were driving through were just fields with a few houses lining the road. The fields then evolved into small businesses connected by unpainted wooden walkways. Some businesses had neon signs that weren't turned on, but I could clearly read "BEER" or "LIQUOR." As we drove closer into town, we noticed a one-story red building situated only a few yards from the road. A sign had alerted us ...SCHOOL. In back of the school there was a parking lot for teachers and a swimming pool with a high fence around it. As we drove by I could see people swimming—only black-skinned people. I sucked in a breath. I had never seen colored people swimming. It was a colored school. A few miles later, the large courthouse came into view. It was in the middle of the town square, with parking meters out front and shops across the streets. We drove around the square a few times, then stopped at a gas station for directions to our house on Odom Street.

The town wasn't very large, so we found the house without any problem. The two-bedroom house that my father got at a bargain price had been owned by the paper mill company. It wasn't anything like the home we had in Mobile, but it was near the First Baptist Church and the paper mill where my father worked. My mother sighed when she got a glimpse of the house. It was situated on a corner and had steps that went up to a concrete slab porch. A narrow driveway on the side led to a dark, one-car garage with a dirt floor. The backyard had a chain-link fence around it and a clothesline that took up most of the yard. Mother finally said, "The mill said it would paint the outside and do any repairs that it needed." My sister and I looked at each other, and I hoped the inside was better than the outside.

Adjusting to life at age fourteen was difficult enough without adjusting to another new school and friends. We wore our poodle skirts with the starched crinolines underneath and scuff-free saddle shoes or penny loafers with turned-down white socks. The boys wore blue jeans and button-down shirts and often sported their high school sweaters with the big letter B. We went to church; we went to football games; we went to movies. It was typical late '50s teen behavior.

The first few months of that year were spent in the old Bastrop High School while a new one was being built. The old high school, they said, was built in 1927, and everyone was anxious to move into a more modern building. On moving day, we kept our books in our laps as the caravan of buses took us to the long-awaited school. It took us a few days to get used to the two-story building and the smell of the new desks and surroundings. Everyone felt like freshmen trying to find their way to their next classes.

I remember sitting in Latin class conjugating Latin verbs and in geometry class measuring right triangles. Chemistry lab was always a challenge to me since I had to remember not to mix certain chemicals that would cause an explosion. I loved English, where we diagramed sentences, but my favorite class was choir. Music had always been my steadfast companion since I was a little person on a big bench at age five. Lessons had continued, through yelling sessions, beaded doors, and a sleeping teacher at the other towns we'd lived in. When we got settled in Bastrop, my mother found a voice teacher and drove me twenty miles to the city of Monroe for lessons. I sang solos for church and for school performances and was chosen to sing at graduation. My training at the charm school in Mobile had given me experience in how to emote and express the meaning of songs.

Football on Friday nights was an exciting event in this small town. Stores put up school banners in their windows, and flags were flown on car antennas. I was one of the flag twirlers on the pep squad, performing at halftime and marching down the street with the band, pep squad, and cheerleaders for the homecoming parades. All of the activities we participated in were spotlighted in the town's newspaper. And of course not one word was printed about the local colored high school and its students. Now I was beginning to notice that in a definite way.

Still, though I was aware of the color barriers now, I was basically uncaring about them: about changes that were beginning the transformation of the South. While I sang in performances, colored people were chanting and singing songs for equality. While I marched and twirled my baton in parades, colored people were marching in throngs for equality. While I sat in new classrooms with new books, colored people still sat in weather-beaten classrooms with used books, waiting for something better. While I was being baptized in my white church, colored people went to their own churches where they praised God and clung to hope for the equality they already had in God's eyes.

My church continued to be one of the main focuses in my life. The First Baptist Church offered me a solace from the outside world. I continued all of the activities on Sunday and had finally been baptized in the big pool of water that was placed above the choir loft in front of the church. My devotion was sincere and complete.

Finding new friends at this new school was a challenge, but somehow we located each other and bonded. There were eight of us whom we called "the Gang," teenaged girls, inseparable. Saturday nights were often spent at different friends' houses and had what we called pallet parties. No one really had sleeping bags in those days, so we took our pillows and rolled them up in our fuzziest blankets.

During these overnight parties I began to realize how much race did matter. I was white and was supposed to be privileged. It was something palpable, something one could feel walking down a street, where black eyes, some unable to be read, might be watching you from nearby. Did we feel that? There was talk. While we sat on our pallets on Saturday nights eating our potato chips and drinking Coca Cola, we talked about "the other race." Our whole teenaged life was segregated in those days, but we had heard stories. During the 1920s the Ku Klux Klan in Morehouse Parish, which included Bastrop, was one of the largest and strongest racist groups in Louisiana. When the Klan murdered two men in the nearby town of Mer Rouge, the governor asked for federal help. The president sent soldiers into Morehouse Parish, and the Klan was shut down in most of the state. Even so, the Klan met secretly until the mid-1950s. They were probably out there somewhere. We were a bit afraid and wondered how this would affect us. I was a newcomer to this town; these girls had been there forever. I listened.

"Did you ever go by the colored swimming pools in the summer? The grease just floats on top of the water. How awful!" and, "My mother has to pick up my father after the night shift, and she has to drive through shantytown. It is so loud in those bars and the colored people just hang out over the rails drinking and swearing," and, "I'm glad we don't have to drink out of the same water fountain with the colored people. Their side is so dirty." Over on my pallet I kept quiet.

We did know, had seen by now on TV, the story of Rosa Parks, who was told to move to the back of the bus when a white man got on. When she refused, she was arrested for not obeying the driver's seat assignment. I do recall connecting it finally, having disturbing memories of Mobile when I had ridden the city bus to school in eighth grade and the driver forced the colored people to stay behind the yellow line. Still, my questions remained unresolved, and I admit I shrugged a lot off. I was having too much high school fun.

Sometimes we would talk about political events in the state, events and people that we had heard our parents discussing. At one of our overnight sessions, someone mentioned the late Huey P. Long of our state and how her parents thought he was one of the best governors in the United States. "My dad said he would have won the presidential race if he had not been assassinated," said one another friend. Huey P. Long, called the King Fish, was governor of Louisiana from 1928 until 1932. Then he served as a US senator until his assassination in 1935. During his term, he authorized thousands of miles of new roads, more than a hundred new bridges, established public schools with free textbooks and free school buses. But by the time of his death, he had seized more control over the state than any politician in history. He padded voting lists, proposed a gag law that prohibited newspapers to print any criticism of him, and packed the courts with his own cronies. In spite of his corrupt policies, the people loved him and voted for four succeeding governors who supported his doctrine. People still clung to his words to make "Every man a king." That was just the way it was.

One day two of my best friends, Betty Lou and Tommie Rhea, and I came out of the new yellow brick library and stepped onto the cracked sidewalk. The three of us were walking side by side, taking up the whole sidewalk, when a colored man came out of a building. It wasn't the library; here, too, as in Georgetown and elsewhere, blacks did not go into our library. He stepped into our path and then quickly jumped off the sidewalk into the gutter filled with trash. He tucked his head, lowered his eyes, and mumbled, "Sorry."

Tommie said as we walked away, "He didn't have to do that." I raised my eyebrows a little bit. Was she cut from a different cloth from many of the girls here when it came to views around us of "colored?" Tommie had lived out in the country in Bastrop all of her life, and her father was involved with the politics of the town. She had told us that sometime after World War II, a colored man came to their house and asked for work. Her father pointed to a shack in the back of the yard and told him he could stay there. The man stayed for years doing odd jobs and even put on a white jacket to help serve at parties. Tommie spoke fondly of this man and remembered seeing him at her father's funeral but never having seen him again after that. There was thoughtful regret in Tommie's voice when she told me that story. It was new to me in this town. We were just teenagers and didn't realize the strength of cultural dictates of the South, but I sensed in an elementary way that Tommie was able to see beyond those beliefs, and I admired that. Someone else seemed to be uncomfortable with "just the way things are."

The Rose Theatre, across the street from the courthouse, was built in the 1920s in the Arts and Crafts style. People came from all over the area to see the latest shows. The tall glass double doors opened into a large lobby, where white patrons bought their tickets and then pushed the wooden swinging doors into the darkened, first-floor viewing room.

Colored people came to see movies along with whites. In some places in the South, colored people had to step into the alley on the side of the building to buy their tickets. Usually there was a staircase along the outside wall that led to the upper entrance and the balcony. In Bastrop, the colored people lined up outside the marquee and purchased their tickets through a grilled window. The colored ticket booth was placed far enough away so the white people wouldn't mingle with them as they waited to get in. If it was cold or rainy, they huddled under the overhang while they waited to enter the small hall, then climbed a dark stairway to the upper balcony.

We teenagers attended that theatre whenever we had the money, happy to see the latest Gene Kelly or Doris Day movies. On one particular day, curious, I stood up in the white person's section downstairs and looked up in the colored people's balcony. I could see it didn't have regular movie seats but only wooden benches set close together. How could they sit through a whole movie like that?

One Friday night, my girlfriends and I met at the movie house. We pushed the heavy glass doors open and got our tickets at the counter next to the concession stand. People hurried through the swinging doors, and the crowd pushed us into the darkened auditorium. It was so dark that we stumbled and almost fell as we searched for the perfect seat. The balcony hung part of the way over the downstairs seating area. We knew we didn't want to sit underneath the balcony because in that sort of dark area all the local thugs sat and they might hit you... or worse. We didn't want to sit in the seats right on the edge of the balcony either, since the colored people would spit or drop Coca-Cola on you.

Still, that night, the best seats, the ones in the middle of the movie theater, were all taken.

Our next choice was on the side. As soon as we got seated and were waiting for the movie to start, a noise started. At first I thought it was storm or maybe a tornado. Then I realized it was the colored people in the balcony stomping their feet. Popcorn started flying and people began shouting. A man with a flashlight appeared in the balcony and shone the light up and down the rows of wooden benches. I heard shouting and boos and hisses... then quiet.

I didn't know how he calmed the colored people down and didn't know why they had even begun the stomping. Perhaps this was their way of demonstrating their solidarity for those standing up for equality in other parts of the South. It was the first time I noticed pushback, a sort of popcorn mini-demonstration against the white system. None of my friends worked at the movie house, and I didn't know anyone who did, but I hoped if I ever worked there I wouldn't have to supervise the balcony.

One of the activities of teenagers on Friday and Saturday nights in this small town was driving around the courthouse looking for other groups who were driving around doing the same thing. We would laugh and wave and see whose car could make it around the courthouse first. Gas wasn't that expensive in those times, and each of us would chip in ten cents to fill the driver's gas tank. When it was my turn to drive, I was always afraid my parents would check the gas gauge to see how far I had driven. They wouldn't have approved of this teenaged rumbling about.

One night, on one of our loops around the courthouse, a car full of boys from out of town pulled up to us, rolled down a window, and shouted, "Is Mary Jane in town?" I looked at my friends in the car and asked, "Who is Mary Jane?" We were so naïve that we didn't know Mary Jane was marijuana. The out-of-towners revved up the motor of their car and sped, laughing, around the corner, leaving us a little shaken up.

However, we weren't so naïve that we didn't know the popular music of the day. The Teen Age Center that we called the TAC Room was a gathering place for Bastrop High School students. Boys flocked around the pool tables and watched sports in the TV room. High school couples would dance on the big wooden floor to the music on the jukebox. Live bands would play at seasonal dances. For days girls would be in a tizzy, planning the outfits they were going to wear if a boy asked them for a date. When we hit the dance floor, we moved to music by Chuck Berry, Johnny Mathis, Ray Charles, Pat Boone, Doris Day, Fats Domino, and The Drifters.

Elvis Presley created a new stage for teenage music—for the world, really. He was virtually unknown when he stopped in Bastrop for a concert in 1955 after performing at the Louisiana Hayride in Shreveport. He would often stop at the local restaurant, and girls would swoon and sit at the same table where he had sat the night before. I only heard other girls talk about watching this new singer with black hair and skintight pants and wished I could have seen him, too.

In 1956, the drive-in theatre opened on the outskirts of town. If a good movie was being shown, our gang would meet at a friend's house for our pallet party, jump into the car, and head out for the drive-in. Just before we got to the entrance, all of us would get on the floor and cover up with a blanket. The designated driver would pull to the ticket booth and purchase one ticket. We were so jammed together under the blanket that we couldn't help giggling and worried that those giggles might alert the ticket person. I remembered the drive-in in Georgetown and Aunt Christine yelling at the colored people in the shadows.

One time one of us sarcastically asked, "Do you really think he didn't know we were hidden on the floor?" Another one of us said, "Maybe next time we could hide in the trunk of the car." That was vetoed because we thought we might suffocate. Such were the quandaries of teenaged girls lounging on the feather beds of southern life in the late 1950s.

The gang and I lived through the turmoil of high school together. Then, in a flash, we separated, each of us off to different colleges. This was the end of my *Gone With the Wind* days, in more than one way.

The Bastrop Flag Twirling Team. I'm in the middle. I can't recall if we could smell the famous Bastrop odor in this field or not.

The Bastrop Bamettes leading the annual Cotton Festival parade. I'm on the right. The town's main street can be seen along the road in this fuzzy old newspaper clipping.

I always enjoyed singing and especially being in the All-State Chorus in 1957. Here I am singing "Stars Fell on Alabama," though I was now in Louisiana. I stuck with music and it led me into teaching the subject.

The Rose Theater is on the National Register of Historic Places. Lots of teen-aged shenanigans went on there when I and my friends attended, along with the viewing of thrillers, westerns, and romantic movies. Racial tensions were also present.

LOUISIANA STATE UNIVERSITY
UNDERGRADUATE AND
GRADUATE SCHOOLS

1958-1963

LSU DAYS

I have said that education was a priority in our family. My father went to LSU in the 1920s then took many correspondence courses. He read a lot of technical books and all the newspapers he could get his hands on. Restlessly, he pursued knowledge all the days of his life, listening to the radio and then the TV, seeking out historical knowledge of places we lived in and taking us on trips to broaden our education.

My mother went only through tenth grade, but I often heard her say, "I should have finished school. It was my own fault." She tried to enlighten herself by going to local concerts and musical events. It was a conscious effort for her. In the 1950s, our entire family would get dressed in our best Sunday clothes and go to the local high school for cultural events. I remember sitting in the hard auditorium chairs and wishing I was back at home with my cat. It was torture for me, but my sister seemed to love it. Once my mother went to the high school and took a class on how to wrap presents. She was so proud that she was able to get a "graduation" certificate from a high school.

It was always assumed that my sister and I would go to college. The only choice we had was where we would go. My sister went to a Christian college in Greenville, South Carolina, and later graduated from the University of Alabama. It was 1958 and my turn to decide. My mother wanted me to go to a Christian school, but I got a scholarship to Louisiana State University in Baton Rouge, and as far as I was concerned, that settled it. I was determined to go LSU but also surprised that my parents ultimately consented to send their "protected" southern girl miles away from home. Off I went, full of hope and with a suitcase of a few sweaters and skirts and three pairs of shoes.

On the first day of freshman orientation, we were grouped together according to our intended major. In those days at LSU, professors served as tour guides for new freshman. I was enrolled in the music school, so I was with the group assigned to Dr. Jordon, a piano professor. He was over six feet tall and had long, gangly arms. His fingers hung limply on those extended hands. He reminded me of a gorilla, but I said nothing until he called roll. When he came to my name, he looked down and asked, "Did it ever bother you that you are so short?" What? Here I was, a 5´1″, seventeen-year-old girl wondering what to say. But I looked up into this stranger's eyes and answered emphatically, "I never thought about it until now." He became my piano professor for two years and told the faculty that I was the most "improved" student he had ever had except for a Chinese student he taught in the past. Even though I wasn't a piano major, I still had to take two years of piano in order to graduate. I was thrilled with his assessment and realized this tall man had confidence in me, short as I was.

All of the freshmen and sophomore girls had to live in dormitories. Most of the rooms held two girls, but there were some that housed four girls. If a parent had enough money, their daughter could have a private room with bath. I was one of the girls with a roommate and had to share the large shower room down the hall. This took some time for me to get used to, since I hadn't had a roommate for seven years and had shared a bathroom only with my sister and parents.

My freshman roommate was from Abbeville and had so many clothes that she brought in a rolling rack to hang them on. Girls weren't allowed to wear dungarees (the denim version of today's jeans) unless they were going bowling or skating, so most of clothes that we wore were skirts and blouses. I didn't have many clothes, so most of mine fitted in the small closet and two dresser drawers. Over the top of the closet was a small shelf where we stored bulky or miscellaneous items. Whenever we needed something from up there, we had to be very careful when we pulled anything down because the big Louisiana cockroaches came flying down on our heads and faces. If we told the housemother that these monsters were in our closet, she would instruct the cleaning women to spray the entire room with a strong bug spray that was worse than the roaches.

A Catholic girl from south Louisiana who spoke with a French Cajun dialect lived at the end of the hall in a private room. She was small, like me, and had thick, bushy black hair that hung to her waist. I had never seen anyone with that much hair. Her black eyes and olive-colored skin set her off from the rest of us. She was very shy and stayed in her room most of the time, even when the rest of us in the hall had group eating binges. One day, a group of girls were gathering around the end of the hall but scattered when they saw me.

My roommate dragged me into the Cajun girl's room and in a whisper said, "Look what we did." On the dresser was a note that said, "Cut your hair, or else." On top of the note was a pair of scissors and a lock of long black hair. I was shocked and asked why they did that. The answer was, "That's to help her. Maybe now she will cut her hair." Then I asked how they got her hair. She said, "We sneaked in when she was asleep and cut it."

I thought about this for the rest of the day and wondered why that group of girls didn't include me in their escapade. Did they know I would never approve of their actions? Had my behavior shown my disdain for this type of harassment? Later, when no one else was around, I sneaked into her room and picked up the note and black hair to discard. I didn't know who the scissors belonged to, so I left them on her dresser. This beautiful Cajun girl with olive skin and black hair stayed for only one semester. I often wished I had been brave enough to confront the culprits in their wrongdoings, but I was just seventeen and not sure of myself.

Most of the boys lived in dorms on the other side of the campus, but some were allowed to live off campus in apartments. My future husband, Butch, lived off campus with a group of guys that majored in forestry. He was from northern Indiana and was used to integration in the schools and public places in the Midwest. After we were married, he told me about one of his roommates, from Shreveport, who had been in our wedding. Butch said, "He always called black people niggers, said they were stupid and if the war could have lasted a little longer the South would have won." He continued, "My roommate always had the Confederate flag flying on his motorcycle with a sign that said, 'The South will rise again.'" So my southern world wasn't the only one where the Civil War was still being fought.

College was a new world, and I adjusted to it just as I had at the many schools I had attended before. Perhaps all those experiences of change had taught me to accommodate and thrive. This took me off on a new journey and set me on unexpected paths. I made it as dormitory treasurer in my freshman year and was selected to be a dorm advisor the next year. I pledged a sorority and helped at various rush parties. But my involvement with my religious beliefs never wavered, and I was elected as secretary of the Baptist Student Union.

The BSU members were involved with all of the religious organizations at LSU and helped at many functions. We traveled to missions in the rural area and institutions and hospitals that housed elderly people. Because I was a pianist, I was often called to play the piano for services for these missions. Many times there were no regular pianos but only "pump organs." I would sit down behind the two-and-a-half-foot-tall organ, place my feet underneath, and play the keyboard while pumping the two pedals at the same time. This was not something I learned from my piano professor, but it was practical and satisfying music.

One of the missionaries who lived near New Orleans invited the BSU members to go to Carville, Louisiana, where the only leper colony in the United States was located. The town, which is sixteen miles south of Baton Rouge, was named for the postmaster of the area and the grandfather of James Carville, the political commentator. We were briefed on a little of the history. Robert Camp, a War of 1812 general, had built his sugar cane plantation in 1859 in this spot along the Mississippi River. He was a flamboyant man who lost his property several times. In 1894, seven people with leprosy were dropped off of a coal barge at this abandoned plantation and told never to leave. This was the start of the first leprosarium in the United States.

We all were apprehensive about this trip but knew if we were going to be good Christians, we would should see firsthand the plight of these people who were plagued with this disease. The facility for the lepers was a long, narrow, white one-story building in back of a regular two-story hospital. The nurses greeted us and gave each of us a long white robe. We were asked us not to touch anything or anyone when we went into the ward. The doctor, who served as our guide, told us about Hansen's disease, commonly known as leprosy, and said that most of these patients, who were very old, had been there all of their lives. There were about twenty male patients, and for some reason, there were no wards for women who had leprosy. He also asked us to try not to stare at any of their disfigurements.

There were several black men at the hospital who were housed in the same ward as the white men even though there were still in effect then many Jim Crow laws prohibiting blacks to intermingle with white people in one way or the other. Hardly a word was spoken as we drove back to campus. Even though we knew a drug had been developed in this facility in 1941 that enabled those afflicted with the disease to lead productive lives, funding was being curtailed. With the decline of new cases, the institute was closed down in 1991. Today, the National Hansen's Disease Museum is located on that old site at Carville, part of a national historic district, and treatment for Hansen's is given at Baton Rouge.

The boring routine of classes and studying remained. Math was my downfall, but I loved English and science. The majority of my time was spent either in the newly opened library or the music building, where my favorite and influential teacher gave voice lessons. Dr. Loren Davidson encouraged me to reach beyond the everyday life of the campus. I sang many solos for community organizations, was in the ESSO Community Choir of Baton Rouge, and was chosen to perform for LSU's 100th Homecoming Show. This show was taken to the LSU campus in New Orleans and then to the State Capitol, where we performed for the state legislators. Performing was exhilarating, but I realized that instead of performance, I had a talent for teaching. This was to be my "calling."

Everything continued at the same pace at LSU, even though laws were implemented to help the colored, now usually called blacks. *Brown vs. Board of Education* had been passed in 1954, but Louisiana amended its constitution to state that all public schools would be operated separately for white and black children. Several black graduate students were already enrolled in master's programs at LSU, and a black undergraduate male enrolled in 1953. However, he was harassed and intimidated constantly, so he dropped out later that year.

Louisiana was stubborn about any moves toward integration. It seemed to be racing backward instead of forward, or at least jogging in place as far as desegregation went. There were many Jim Crow laws still on the books in Louisiana going back to the 1800s: 1894–intermarriage between white persons and persons of color prohibited; 1908–unlawful for whites and blacks to buy and consume alcohol on the same premises; 1914–all circuses, shows, and tent exhibitions required to provide two ticket offices with individual ticket sellers and two entrances to the performance for each race. The same year I entered college, Louisiana passed a law stating that all blood to be used for transfusion had to be labeled "Caucasian," "Negroid," or Mongoloid" to show race. If it was not labeled, then it was not to be used. Even in 1960, a law was passed that the race of all candidates running for any office had to be shown on the ballots.

In spite of this, momentum for change could not be stopped. These days brought in the sit-ins and the Freedom Riders. Most of us at LSU were so busy with our own lives that the only time we heard about this was when we were at the movies and saw news. We didn't have TVs in our dormitories, but caught up with the news when we went home on the weekends or on vacation.

But change went forward, even if we as college students let the changes go by largely unnoted, or noticed only in passing. 1960 was called the year of the student-led lunch counter sit-ins. The fast food providers like McDonalds had just started opening in the country, and only a few suburban malls existed. Downtown was still the main shopping district, where lunch counters provided food for workers and shoppers. It was estimated there were more than 30,000 lunch counters in drugstores and public buildings like Woolworth and Kresge's in the country. It was at a Kresge lunch counter in Baton Rouge in 1960 that seven students from Southern University in Baton Rouge, a black university, participated in a sit-in. They were arrested and charged with disturbing the peace. The next day, nine students from SU were arrested. These sixteen students were expelled from the university, which prompted 3,500 students to walk out of class and march to the capital. This boycott evolved into mass withdrawal of students from the university.

All of this was happening around me only a few miles south of my school, while I just thought about my studies, music, football, and boys. I fault myself now for being oblivious to something that in my heart I had already seen was wrong. I guess none of us talked about the racial turmoil since it didn't affect us. Ironically, I thought about the starving children in Africa and even posted a picture of emaciated African children on my bulletin board. But I was unaware of the plight of the black children in the United States. We all stayed in our own little bubble. It protected us from reform. My mind knew the societal mores about race were horrible; my own experience had confirmed that. But my heart had not accepted the truth: race was not a factor in how we should value men and women. What I'd grown up with was wrong.

That was about to change. I was heading for my moment of full recognition and separation forever from Dixie's feather bed of intolerance.

INTERLOCHEN

It was 1960, and I was nearing the end of my second year of college. June was creeping closer, and I had to decide what to do for the summer. I needed a break from school, and I certainly didn't want to spend another summer at home in Bastrop, Louisiana. There were several flyers posted on the music building's bulletin board about jobs at lodges at national parks and other venues. One stood out: a student counselor job at Interlochen Music Camp near Traverse City, Michigan.

I didn't ask my parents' permission. I simply filled in the application and mailed it the next week. When I told my parents about my acceptance, my father seemed proud that his little petite southern girl would venture thousands of miles away, but my mother worried that I would be away for a whole summer without her protection.

That June, I packed a few things and my parents made the long drive to Yankee land, where I would live in a rustic cabin and supervise high school girls. The day before we arrived in Michigan, my father asked me, "What will you do if you have any colored girls in your cabin?"

I asked, "Why do you ask that?" It never occurred to me that the camp would be integrated and I would have to supervise black girls. He then said, "You know there will probably be other children and counselors that are colored. They will be coming from all over the country." I was surprised at his question and my naivety. With a quivering voice I answered, "I guess I will treat them like everybody else."

Not another word was spoken about that, but I realized my father understood what I might be facing...the world of integration. My father turned off the highway and onto a rough, pine-forested road that led to the rustic gates of the camp. We found the main building and pushed through the mingling campers, parents, and counselors. After getting all of the paperwork filled out, my parents said goodbye, and I was on my own in this beautiful land.

I found my way to my cabin, where I sat on my sagging bed and pulled out the folder that they gave me. Pictures showed Joseph Maddy, who founded the camp in 1928 with high dreams for honoring and furthering music, which he loved above all things. Interlochen was an eight-week summer camp, but Joe had plans to develop it into a full-fledged school called the Interlochen Arts Academy. The camp also had two-week summer sessions for high school students from Michigan. Those All-State Campers were to be my students.

The information continued with a map showing nearby Traverse City. The city was known for its annual Cherry Festival. In spring, the area becomes alive when cherry orchards burst into full blossoming flowers. Summer transforms the area into all thing cherry— cherry pie, cherry drinks, cherry-decorated clothes and cherry stands piled high with the sweet juicy fruit of two kinds: dark cherries for eating out of the hand and pie cherries. People come from all over the country in midsummer to celebrate a week of cherry-laden festivities. We counselors came to know this town only a little through trips in our spare time.

The outdoor Interlochen Bowl was in the center of the camp. That's where audiences sat on row after row of hard-backed wooden benches watching dancers, singers, and orchestral and individual performances. In the background, they could see the camp's two shimmering lakes nestled among the towering white and balsam pines. The dining room and the camp store were next to the bowl, with different-sized buildings for classes nearby. Campers had to walk down the narrow dirt road to the wooden cabins scattered among the trees. It was midsummer, but the temperature was cool. I did not miss the blistering heat of Louisiana in the summer.

I spread the map out on the floor and found the All-State beach. One of my assignments for the summer was to be a lifeguard where the All-State campers swam during their free time. I had taught beginning swimming to children at LSU and got my Red Cross lifesaving certificate, so I planned to survey this waterfront closely before all the campers arrived.

The first meeting of the staff was scheduled later that night, so I had time to put my small trunk under the bed and put on my uniform. All of the campers, employees, and guest performers wore neat but rather rugged camp uniforms. The boys wore navy blue corduroy trousers, and the girls wore white knee socks and navy blue knickers that buttoned below the knees. Everyone wore light blue shirts during the week and white ones on

Sundays. No one really complained about the uniforms. Later, if we happened to go into Traverse City in our uniforms, everyone recognized us as the kids from the music camp, and we were proud to be known as "the blue corduroy knicker campers."

We were to be there eight weeks. At the end of each two-week session, we had a bonfire sing-a-long with all of the All-State students. Usually, the male counselors and their boys built the fire in the afternoon and "officially" invited all of the girls over to their side of the camp. We had lots of singing, marshmallow roasting, and "kumbaya-ing." I loved it.

Faster than I could realize, the last session of the summer was coming to a close, and even the counselors were a little teary eyed at the prospect of leaving. We were all sitting cross-legged in the dirt at that last campfire with the kids when one of the counselors suggested we all join hands and dance around the fire. Laughing and giggling burst out as all of the campers and counselors clasped hands. I held my hand out, and a small black hand fell into it. I looked down at this young black male camper and panicked. All of a sudden, I had a hard time breathing and choked when I tried to sing. This was the first time I had ever held hands with a black person. In the back of my mind, a signal went off: "You are not supposed to socialize with a colored person." I followed the rest of the circle around the fire while trying to understand what I was feeling. Finally, the song was over, and I sat down away from the others, conflicted.

At that moment, we all looked into the sky and saw the aurora borealis as it flashed and swooped across the sky. It was green that night, maybe green with envy at our happiness in this place. It seemed like a giant hand being compressed in pain as it stretched, relaxed, then stretched again. Not a sound was heard except the crackling and hissing of the fire. I looked over at this small, black twelve-year-old boy whose hand had fallen into mine while we danced around the fire. He was looking into the sky just like the rest of us. His color didn't matter. He was like the aurora borealis, adding hidden color to the sky of our world.

I felt so small. There was that huge miracle making itself clear to me, and I was powerless to do anything about it. I couldn't turn my eyes away from the truth.

The next morning, we said goodbye to all of the campers, checked the cabins, and freed our minds from worry. It was now our last day, and we would celebrate it together as friends. The All-State counselors and staff were going to take off that afternoon and go to the mouth of a small stream named Otter Creek that flowed into gigantic Lake Michigan for a party. We were determined to have a good time.

All morning and early afternoon it rained, a gentle rain. By midafternoon a glimpse of sun peeped through, even though storms were predicted. I wanted to take a walk along a back road before I met the other counselors. The countryside was alive again. All of the trees were refreshed, their bright greens blending with the still, dark sky. There was a little cherry stand with a friendly man standing behind the counter, and I can still remember the taste of the cherries that he sold. MY MICHIGAN! I felt. I wandered to the beach where I had spent many hours guarding the swimmers. Thick fog covered the wooden pier jutting out over the water. The beach was deserted, and a sign on the lifeguard house said "Beach Closed." I took a deep breath and said goodbye to that part of the summer. Then I found the other counselors back at the cabins, and we piled into cars and drove to Lake Michigan. There she was, my Michigan, spread out as shimmering water this time. All that was left to remind us of the predicted storm were the few clouds melting away with the setting sun.

We ate steaks that could melt in your mouth if they stayed there a few seconds longer, downed cherry pie, and licked sticky toasted marshmallows off our fingers. I stopped and looked over my shoulder. . .the sky was afire with blazing red embers that looked like the dying fire we had burning on the beach. As the sun began sinking into the lake, we watched in silence, half expecting to hear a hissing noise as it dropped and see a cloud of steam rising from the lake. Instead, there was a flash of green. It lingered just a little longer than usual, then vanished with the sun.

As I lay on my cot in the cabin that last night, the rain came. It was not a gentle rain that could caress the ground and sink in immediately, but the angry kind that spat on everything, splashed, and made dark pools. Soon its anger subsided and gentled, as if the falling drops were asking for forgiveness. It was then I realized my journey of positive acceptance of others, no matter the color of their skin, was underway. Those last two nights of farewell opened the sky for me, too.

The six male and seven female counselors in the All-State Division that summer were from all over the country...Texas, San Francisco, St. Louis, Iowa, Detroit, Chicago, several from Michigan, and then me, from Louisiana. My fellow counselors in just eight weeks had helped shape my life. We had shared stories, discussed politics, and talked about our hopes and dreams. Most of them would never have been hesitant to hold hands with someone of another race. They dug into my conscience and showed me how to look at the way things are and how things should be. That summer was the start of the path I wanted to follow.

When I got back to Dixie, I wrote an account of my eight-week journey, but I never told any of my friends about my hand-holding with that camper. The sit-ins were continuing, and the LSU students were still floating around in their bubbles. I had changed, but ol' Dixie's feather bed was just the same.

MOVING ON IN MY EDUCATION

I was back at LSU and smiled whenever I remembered the summer at Interlochen. I could see the "other world," larger than what I had known, and wanted to become a part of it.

As a junior and then completing my last year, I could note that turmoil seemed to be everywhere in the South, not just in Louisiana. Everyone had heard about George Wallace of Alabama, but now I was paying attention. I began to seek news about him specifically. He was preparing to run for governor of Alabama on a strict segregationist platform. He threatened to confront the federal government over forced integration of the schools. Though I didn't know it at the time, Wallace would be a four-time candidate for president of the United States, a man who would say "Segregation now, segregation tomorrow, segregation forever," and who would block the path of two black students who were registering at the University of Alabama. All of that was for the future; as a student at LSU in the early 1960s, I could see him snaking through the grass towards fist-raising defiance to a new age of tolerance that was just beginning to make itself felt.

The problem of vacations and weekends loomed over my head. I hated going home and tried to find ways of not visiting there, even though I felt guilty when my mother begged me to come home. The minute I would get out of my car, the atmosphere in that segregated and confining town would settle on me like the smell of the paper mill. I felt like I was being strangled. The church I had loved and gone to in high school didn't help, since the new pastor's suffocating sermons were only about fire and brimstone. It was about this time that I began questioning religion and the way I understood it before I went to college. In high school, my friends and I never talked about religion, and I had never been exposed to any other way of looking at Christianity except through the teachings of the Southern Baptists. Now I began to doubt the role of all organized churches. My faith remained steadfast, but I was disappointed at some of the hypocrisies that so-called highly religious church members flaunted, especially about integration. I pored over books about Christianity as well as those of other religions and found the world is connected through one common element, and that is love. The essence of Christianity dawned on me, non-sectarian and very large, and although I never became a regular churchgoing Christian again, it stayed in my heart all the rest of my life and motivated a lot of my actions and philosophy.

John F. Kennedy had come upon the world stage, elected when I was graduating in 1962. His enthusiasm inspired the youth of the country, and many of us now thought about joining the Peace Corps. Some of my friends and I began discussing politics and the upcoming election, but most students were so busy with their own circle of friends and completion of college that their individual beliefs stayed locked up and hidden.

My Southern Baptist mother and I were at odds with each other. She knew I was moving in a direction opposite in some ways to the culture I'd grown up in. I spouted JFK's words to her: "Our most basic common link is that we all inhabit this planet. We breathe the same air. We all cherish our children's future. And we are all mortal." And, "Change is the law of life. And those who look only to the past or present are certain to miss the future."

Her comments were still the same: "The colored people are just one jump down out of the trees. It says so in the Bible." And, "Kennedy is Catholic, and if he is elected president, the Pope will tell him what to do, and he will have colored people marrying white people." It was so simplistic. I could only shake my head.

Finally, in 1962 graduation came...along with the whispers around us of an approaching war in Vietnam. On graduation day, as we stood in line to get our diplomas, I looked around and wondered if there was a war coming whether I would ever see some of my friends again. I noticed some young men in the audience in full military uniform and wondered, "If they go to war, will they even come back?"

I had my own decisions to make: to go to work in the fall or accept a graduate assistantship in the music department. My father left the decision to me, but I think secretly he wanted me to continue my studies at LSU, which I did.

I had met a graduate student who was getting a master's degree in social work and decided to share an apartment with her. We found a garage apartment that was within walking distance of the school and that we could afford. It had one large open room, one bedroom, a tiny kitchen, and an even tinier bathroom, but that was all we needed. We shared chores and took turns cooking. She was a much better cook than I and taught me how to make some wonderful Cajun dishes. I had my mother's old pressure cooker and decided to cook some beans that would last for a week. Even though I had watched her use this cooker many times, I forgot to let it cool down before opening it. I pushed and pulled at the lid, and finally it popped open, spewing red beans all over the kitchen and ceiling. We laughed, but I was the one who had to scrape the beans off the walls.

One afternoon, I heard a knock on the door. Outside was a dark-skinned girl with a long colorful dress. The flowing garment was draped over her shoulder and looped around her waist. Her coal black hair was pulled back in a braid, and a red dot on her forehead between her eyebrows accented her dark brown eyes. I stood there waiting for one of us to say something. She finally said with a strange accent, "I live in the apartment downstairs and thought I would come to meet you." So my new views were being put to the test.

During that year, my roommate and I got to know this young Hindu woman from India. Loshna's fiancé wanted her to come to America to study engineering and to learn about our culture. We had many conversations about life in India as well as life in America.

Once, she asked me, "How do you get your legs so smooth and free from hair?" I went upstairs to my apartment and got a razor and showed her how we shaved our legs. She told me about the red dot that she wore on her forehead. Pointing to the spot between her eyebrows she said, "This area represents the subconscious mind where negative thoughts may enter." Leaning over so I could see, she continued, "We paint the red bindi decoration there to block the negative thoughts."

Loshna showed us how the Hindu women wrapped and wore a sari. She wore a long petticoat and draped four to nine meters of unstitched material around her body. The blouses that she wore were either backless or in a style with a halter neck. I couldn't imagine having to do all of this draping and dressing each morning. It seemed so complicated, but must have felt so freeing when she walked down the street. I often thought about this brave lady and wondered what other people thought about her. Her dark skin and her colorful sari made her stand out in this university. I was proud to know her and hoped she didn't feel any of the prejudice around us.

LSU was still a white undergraduate university. A few black students had graduated earlier with master's degrees, but the undergraduate school was still segregated. I had never been to school with any black students. My entire southern life had been one of whites only. I was a grown woman with a college degree, so this was to be a revelation and a disappointment to me.

The graduate school classes were small, no more than ten students in each, and a few black students had been allowed into grad school again. In one of these classes, I struck up a friendship with a black lady. She was staying with her parents while her husband was deployed abroad. Both she and her husband were graduates of Southern University in Baton Rouge, where he had immediately signed up for the army after graduation. Carolyn was a tall lady with beautiful chocolate skin and short black hair that was smoothed back behind her ears. Her smile and cheerfulness filled the room when she entered. At first I felt the old apprehension about being in a class with a black person, but within a few days I was able to accept her fully as a fellow student. Ingrained patterns, cultivated over years, are hard to leave behind even though Interlochen had changed me. As time went on, we began comparing notes and decided to study together for exams.

Carolyn would drive over to my apartment and set her books on the table. I poured Cokes over ice for us and made a large bowl of popcorn. Then we settled back in the hard chairs to cram for exams. We began discussing our notes, drinking our ice-cold Cokes and reaching for the popcorn. I watched as if it was a scene from a movie, her black hand digging into the popcorn next to my white hand. I smiled when I realized what I was seeing: the demonstration of an alteration in my own perspective.

We spent many hours together studying and talking about family and life experiences. It was if we had known each other in another life... a life not filled with segregation. Still, there were borders around my "integration."

An old black woman, who cleaned the floors and bathrooms in the music building, was always at her station each morning. She looked to be a hundred years old as she pushed her mop and bucket of water over the marble floors. Between classes, she leaned against the walls while students rushed by, then resumed cleaning after the tardy bell had rung. Each day people, all of us, walked past her, and each day the same people never seemed to notice her. It was as if she was a stone statue placed along those marble walls. Even the professors seemed to rush past her to their assigned lecture rooms or offices. As I waited in the lobby before class one day, I noticed this old woman was sitting on the marble steps to the balcony. Her bucket of water was pushed against the wall, while her head was resting on the handle of the mop. She was sweating and breathing hard. People rushed on by, but one professor, Dr. Timm, approached her.

He touched her shoulder, and when she looked up, he asked, "How are you today? Are you OK?" I couldn't hear anything else, but in a few minutes he helped her get up and they left. My heart went out to her, and I realized I had never acknowledged her. I was ashamed and wondered if she had been there when I first entered the building my freshman year, five years ago. Why did I notice her now? Maybe I was beginning to see through the veil of prejudice and discrimination, even though I still was not able to fully act on my new perceptions.

My graduate conducting class had only five students... three white male students, one black male, and me. The professor was known to have a quick temper, so I was very nervous about this class. Each day we met in a small downstairs classroom and listened to lectures about different styles of conducting. We practiced conducting while we listened to various classical compositions on scratchy vinyl records. The professor had each of us take turns in front of the class and conduct a recorded orchestral composition of his choice. We stepped up on the small platform, placed the musical scores on the stand, and conducted the score in time to the recording. Then he would critique us. He was very nice to me and offered helpful suggestions. It seemed to me that he was this way with all of us except the one black male student. Whenever it was his turn, the professor would shout at him and make him do the same passage over and over again. All of the other classmates and I would slide down in our chairs and stare at the floor so we wouldn't have to watch this harassment.

One day after class I said to the black student, "I am so sorry about how he treated you." He looked surprised. I don't know if he was surprised that I noticed or surprised because he himself didn't feel he was being harassed. Perhaps he expected the extreme criticism. Was he warned this would happen, or was he used to this type of treatment? Perhaps he did not wish to be singled out—to have anything noticed about him. Or maybe this didn't bother him as much as it bothered me. That was the only class I had with this black student, and I never had another chance to talk with him about this situation.

THE 1960s ROLL ON

Before graduating from LSU, my roommate introduced me to a guy from northern Indiana, which we jokingly called Yankee land. He was called "Butch" by everybody, but his real name was Ervin. We had often double dated and did crazy things like run up and down the Louisiana State Capitol steps at night, then jump up and down on Huey Long's grave at the capitol. Butch and I would often sit on the levee of the Mississippi River in Baton Rouge and watch the muddy water flow downstream. There was always something fun and interesting to do together.

The schools were all integrated when he was in high school, and all of the team sports that he had been on were integrated as well. He had heard about the Ku Klux Klan and its influence in the 1920s in Indiana, but he had grown up in a different era. The only time he heard any of his relatives speak negatively about another class of people was when they would say, "That's those dumb Polocks," referring to the Polish people that lived nearby. He was aware of the South's strong rejections of integration but had never experienced racial prejudice intensely until he came south. After graduation, he moved back to Indiana to attend Valparaiso Law School, and I stayed at LSU. Those were the days when the phone companies charged extra money for each long-distance call, so we were limited in the amount of time we spent on the phone. Instead, we wrote letter after letter, which I still today have tied up with a blue silk ribbon.

Finally, we married in 1963 and moved to Valparaiso, Indiana, far away from our Louisiana memories in college. But we were making new memories. We lived in a little two-room cottage in the middle of an apple orchard, surrounded by lilac bushes. I had never been in an apple orchard, and when a ripe apple would drop down on the roof of our cottage during the night, I would jump at the booming noise, wondering if something was trying to get into the house.

My husband had gone to high school in Hammond, Indiana, and had relatives in Gary. One Saturday we decided to drive to Gary for a family reunion.

I had my husband stop the car at a grocery store a few miles from his aunt's house to pick up a pie for dessert. I climbed out of the car and began walking down the middle of the sidewalk. I came face to face with four high-school-aged black girls taking up the entire sidewalk. As they came closer, I panicked, an ingrained reaction because they were not getting off the sidewalk like blacks did in Louisiana. I quickly stepped into the trash-filled gutter and waited until they left. They hadn't said anything to me or even made any kind of intimidating gesture, but I was shaking as I stepped back on the sidewalk.

When I returned with the pie, I told my husband about the incident. He was relieved that I wasn't hurt, but he chuckled under his breath because he realized that this little southern wife of his had a lot to learn. This was not the segregated South.

That same year, my husband was in a law class when a booming voice came over the loud speaker: "JFK has been assassinated." I was teaching music in the nearby town of Chesterton and didn't know about it until I got home that afternoon. We sat in our little cottage and watched the reports from Dallas on our little nine-inch black-and-white TV for the next few days and wondered what was going to happen next. The entire world stood still.

The year of our first year of marriage, 1963, was also a time when the civil rights movement grew ever stronger with protests, sit-ins, and demonstrations. Again in May the entire world stood still as it watched the beatings, high-pressure fire hoses, police dogs, and arrests in Birmingham, Alabama. These events prompted some to repeat Martin Luther King's statement that Birmingham was the most segregated city in the US. King was one of the people who was arrested and jailed in 1963. A quote from his famous letter while he was in jail reads, "Injustice anywhere is a threat to justice everywhere...Whatever affects one directly, affects all indirectly."

The Birmingham riots were prompted by bombings that targeted black civil rights leaders. Witnesses saw police place bombs that were likely planted by members of the Ku Klux Klan. The United States government sent federal troops for the first time to control the violence that was connected to these riots.

But more violence erupted when four young black girls were killed when a bomb exploded in the Sixteenth Street Baptist Church. These innocent Christian black girls were in the basement of the church changing their choir robes and anticipating going home to be with their parents.

As I watched these events on TV, I remembered my days as a child in South Carolina. I thought of my relatives. They were all gone now, scattered from Arkansas to Alaska, and I wondered if their views remained the same or had moved forward with changing times.

In 1964, my husband was offered a job in Georgia, in Atlanta. Life took a turn, and we were thrust back into Dixie. Atlanta was a beautiful city, rapidly expanding, with so many cultural things to see and do. Street billboards boasted that it was a city "too big to hate." Even so, racial strife existed, but it didn't seem to affect us since we lived on the north side of town. Here I noted, with some chagrin, signs posted that said "white residents only." Several subdivisions wouldn't allow blacks even to enter after dark, and the homeowners paid a security company to patrol the area at night to enforce the restriction. Was I ready, though, "reconstructed" as I was, to live in an integrated neighborhood? That was a question I wasn't prepared to answer.

We went to plays and concerts in the city. I performed in Ionesco's play *The Rhinoceros* and the Broadway musical *Stop the World, I Want to Get Off* in downtown Atlanta to an all-white audience. We ate at wonderful restaurants and prayed at our non-integrated church. We visited Stone Mountain Park near Atlanta and saw the largest Confederate memorial carving in the world, which depicts the Confederate generals Stonewall Jackson and Robert E. Lee, and the president of the Confederacy, Jefferson Davis. This memorial had been the site of many Ku Klux Klan rallies and meetings since 1915, gatherings which continued until 1960, when the state outlawed them. My husband and I remembered Martin Luther King's "I Have A Dream" speech in 1963, in which he said, "Let freedom ring from Stone Mountain Georgia."

We asked ourselves, "How much longer will people continue to pay homage to that horrible time when our country was split in half?" But it wasn't only whites who hadn't fully accepted integration; old patterns died hard for our black neighbors, also, and resentment, too. One night my husband and I went to a bar on the black side of the city where the best jazz was being played. It was early when we got there, and we got lost in time. About nine o'clock we looked up and saw that all of the white couples had left and only black people filled the room. We had been told this was not a safe place for white people and we should be out of the area by eight o'clock. Nothing happened to us, but we thought it was a shame that the color of a person's skin should dictate where you could go and be safe.

A monumental moment for this era happened July 2, 1964, when President Johnson signed the Civil Rights Act, stating restaurants and public places could not discriminate against minorities. Lester Maddox, a restaurant owner in Atlanta, came to national attention when he refused to serve three black Georgia Tech students in his Pickrick Restaurant. When the students entered, Mattox waved a pistol at them and shouted, "You no good devils! You dirty Communists!" Customers who agreed with him grabbed axe handles from the front of the store and waved them at the students. Maddox called these handles "Pickrick drumsticks" and sold them in his souvenir shop to symbolize his resistance to the civil rights movement. That night on TV we watched these white men take wooden handles and swing at the black people. We saw some white people standing outside the restaurant. They seemed to be shouting at the blacks. Some months later, we read that a judge ordered Maddox to end discrimination or close the restaurant. We were shocked when Maddox chose to close the restaurant rather than serve blacks.

The newspapers never gave up in their coverage of Lester Maddox in the mid-1960s. One night we read the latest on Maddox and saw he was running for governor of Georgia with the support of the Ku Klux Klan. No one won the majority of votes in that election, and according to Georgia law, the legislature would make the final decision. Even though the popular vote was Howard "Bo" Calloway with 47.07% and Maddox with 46.85%, the legislators decided to choose the segregationist, Maddox.

It seemed like the entire South, not just isolated areas, was now on fire with protests and riots. There was the Bloody Tuesday in Tuscaloosa, Alabama, in June 1964; the four-day riot in Summerville, Georgia, and others. In March of 1965, six hundred people, led by John Lewis and other activists, assembled in Selma, Alabama, and began their march to Montgomery.

As they approached the Pettus Bridge over the Alabama River, they were blocked by Alabama state troopers and local police. When the marchers refused to turn around, the officers shot teargas into the crowd and began beating the nonviolent protesters with billy clubs and rubber hoses wrapped in barbed wire. This came to be known in history as "Bloody Sunday."

In the fall of 1965, and in the midst of all of this in Georgia and the South, I signed a contract to teach fourth grade in Riverdale, which was ten miles south of Atlanta. This was an ordinary segregated white school in the middle of town. Each morning I drove through Atlanta's rush hour to get to school by 7:30, and every morning before 7:30 the black custodian was there to unlock the doors so the teachers could get in. During recess and lunch, he patrolled the schoolyard, supervising the students. He didn't talk to me much, but when he did, he looked at me through lowered eyes and spoke so softly I could hardly hear him. I mention this because, against what I would have wished, this was the only contact I had with any black person that entire year.

Everyone knew that the South, as well as the entire country, was under federal orders to integrate the schools. Even though the *Brown vs. Board of Education* bill was passed in 1954, it didn't give a timeline for integration or a method as to how the schools were to be integrated. The following year a bill was passed: "integrate with all deliberate speed." However, a decade after the *Brown vs. Board of Education* decision, less than 2% of the schools were integrated.

The superintendent of Clayton County, where I taught, hired me and three other white teachers to be music consultants in the county. Each of us was assigned three white schools and one black school. My fellow teachers and I spoke about the assignment. We told each other that this was probably one way the superintendent and school board could say, "Our schools are integrated."

None of us had ever taught in an integrated school and were apprehensive. In spite of my growing conviction that all people should be treated equally, my childhood milieu still clamored deep in my consciousness. We met in our office on Mondays and spent one day each at our four schools. I remember meeting on the Monday after our first week's assignment and discussing our experiences. One of the music consultants, Betty White, told us, "I got up in front of all these black children and said, 'I am Mrs. White and am your music teacher.'" Betty said she felt so awkward with those remarks and wondered if the children and teachers were as uncomfortable as she was. We were all on fresh, green turf.

My black school was for first through eighth graders. The building was brand new and looked like a typical one-story block building with a nice parking lot and playground for the elementary children. Classrooms lined each side of the long hall on one end of the building, with the principal's office and cafeteria on the opposite end.

On Fridays I went into each classroom for thirty minutes and sang and played instruments with the children. At first, they just sat there and stared at me. These black children must have been as nervous about having a white teacher in their school as I was being a white teacher in their black school. One of my favorite songs to sing with all my early grade students was "Pick-A-Bale of Cotton." I would put the tape in the machine and sing the song with them. After they learned the song, I told them when they heard the word "pick-a-bale" they were to jump down, turn around, and pretend to pick cotton. This had been so much fun with my white students that it never entered my mind this might have been something my black students didn't want to think about, since so many of their parents and grandparents had bad memories of working in the cotton fields. The students stood like statues for the whole song until the black teacher said, "OK children, you know what it's like to pick cotton. Let's pretend." She proceeded to sing the song with me and turned and "picked cotton" with the children. She must have sensed the tension from both the children and me.

The students finally got used to me and without hesitation sang and laughed and played instruments that I brought. I knew I was respected as a teacher when one of the first-grade black teachers approached me as I was walking down the hall. She pulled me aside and confided something she had observed with amusement, "Guess what one of my little girls brought her lunch money in today? A used condom tin."

I laughed with her but was surprised she trusted me enough to treat me as a sister and colleague. Later, when the children lined up to go to lunch, the same teacher called me over and said to the little girl, "Show the music teacher what you put your lunch money in today." The black girl pulled out her "tin" full of lunch coins and smiled at her black teacher and me, then skipped on down the hall to lunch.

A young, nice-looking black man who always wore a coat and tie was the choral teacher for the eighth graders as well as the high school. One day he called me into the cafeteria where the piano was located. He asked me to look at some music he was using for the high school and give him my opinion. Not since graduate school at Louisiana State University had I been in contact with any minority musicians. We stood in front of the piano and sang while he played the accompaniment. It was only one song, but a revelation! At that sharing moment I never saw him in my mind as being black. He was just another teacher. I was shocked at that strange feeling and wondered again, "I really know this and now I experience it: Why does skin color matter? We are all here to care about the children."

I always tried to eat lunch in each of my school's cafeterias so the children and teachers would recognize me and I would recognize them. The first day at my black school, I got in the cafeteria line, paid my money, and sat at a table in back near the door. I looked over the sea of black children's faces and then stared down at my lunch tray. It was filled with turnip greens, cornbread, some type of meat, and some vanilla pudding. I had eaten this type of soul food all of my life and liked it, but I became nauseated at this sight. I shoved a little cornbread in my mouth then left after putting my tray in the rack. My reaction surprised me. Was this a leftover feeling from my segregated days when whites were not supposed to use any plates or utensils that blacks touched? I didn't know if any of the other music consultants would have had this reaction, so I never confided in them.

During those two years and out of my four schools, this black segregated school had the most well-behaved students and the most appreciative teachers of them all.

My husband ran a construction company in Atlanta that built houses for high-income people. When he came home at night, he would sit by the back door and take his shoes and socks off. His socks were white when he left in the morning but were caked with red Georgia mud when he got back home. Red mud was everywhere, on cars, on clothes, and on animals.

If your car happened to go off on the side of the road, there would be no returning, for the car would immediately slide into the slick red clay.

Our son was born in 1967. My husband's mother and stepfather came to visit. I was a first-time mother and nervous at taking care of a newborn. When my mother-in-law suggested we all go out to dinner and leave our two-week-old with a babysitter, I demurred. I asked, "Why can't we take him with us?" but was outnumbered. Then I posed the question to my husband, "Who can we get to sit? Where will we find someone?" Finally, he said, "I'll ask my ditchdigger if his wife will babysit." He had told me about a man whom he employed to dig ditches in the red clay for the footings of the houses he built. The black man showed up early each morning with his entire family, including his wife, who shoveled dirt and mud right alongside him. The first thing the black man did when they came was to set up a four-sided screen canvas a few yards from the construction area. My husband realized he did that so his wife could have a private place to use the bathroom. Before they started work in the morning, the entire family gathered around in a circle and prayed. Then again at lunch, they offered a prayer before eating. I remembered meeting this black woman when she and her husband came to our house the day after we brought our son home from the hospital. They had gone home after digging in that Georgia red mud, cleaned up, and made the trip back across town just to see our newborn son.

That night, my husband drove to the other side of town and picked the woman up. When he brought her into the house, I remembered how large she was and noticed how strong her arms were, probably made that way from all the physical work she did. Her clean cotton flowered dress was covered by an apron that looked like one my mother used to wear. Before we headed out the kitchen door, I turned and looked at her and felt a deep understanding of all the black women that raised white children as their own. This black woman was cradling our white son in her arms as if this were a natural thing all mothers, black or white, know how to do. The love of mothers transcends all colors.

The summer of 1967 became known as the "summer of love." Over 100,000 young people of every race and color converged in San Francisco to protest the Vietnam War and to promote the value of people over things. As the war on the other side of the ocean was ramping up, people thought of jungles, napalm, and the draft but the hippies handed out flowers to people and held up peace symbols. At first this gathering was peaceful, but as more people came to the city, more illnesses, filth, and crime came with them, and by the fall most of the Flower Children had moved to rural communities.

That summer brought in the Peace Movement, the Farm Workers Movement, the Animal Rights Movement, the Anti-War Movements, and many more. The Black Power Movement also had its birth during that time. It stood for racial pride, self-sufficiency, and equality for all blacks. The Black Panthers were part of that movement. The group believed Martin Luther King's peaceful campaign wasn't working, and they were willing to use violence to get its voice known. We watched on television these black members dressed in black jackets, black pants, black berets, and black sunglasses. They took advantage of California's laws and carried unconcealed guns. They meant to intimidate, and they did.

It seemed the world was caught in a whirlwind and would come crashing down, scattering the broken pieces all across the land. I wondered what kind of world I was bringing my son up in.

LOUISIANA STATE CAPITOL AT BATON ROUGE—36

*Huey P. Long monument (r.)
Governor Long's programs for
the poor included his state's
African Americans and he held
moderate views toward segregation.
He was, however, in no mood to
change the Jim Crow segregation
laws in his state.
I wasn't fully aware of these
elements in the man's career at
the time.*

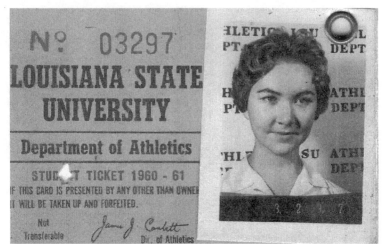

I'm a great supporter of Lousiana State University to this day.

The National Hansen's Disease Museum. We visited the institution as undergraduates.

This poster was on my wall at LSU. Congo babies: symbol for all the starving children in the world. I was becoming alert to others outside my sphere.

My good friend Losh-na with friends. She was the first person of color I came to know.

Kress lunch counter protesters in 1960 in Baton Rouge were somber and determined as they sat to order lunch—which they didn't get. What they really got was credit for starting the young people's part of the Civil Rights movement. Huge demonstrations followed.

At Interlochen between years at college, I'm seated in the middle of things—a good metaphor for me at this point in my life, since I'd always been an involved person. Now I was exposed for the first time to a variety of people and experiences.

Interlochen beach steak fry for the All-State staff at Otter Creek on Lake Michigan. During this end-of-camp time I saw the Northern Lights for the first time and held hands with a "colored" boy. My world was opening up marvelously.

Stone Mountain near Atlanta was purchased in 1958 by the state of George as a memorial to the Confederacy. Erv and I visited the site, with its partially completed relief. We also went to movies at the historic Loew's Grand Theater on Peachtree Street. It was here that Margaret Mitchell's Gone with the Wind had its Atlanta premier in 1939. But our days in the South were limited.

TUCSON 1967–2003

LIFE IN THE DESERT

Always I had had to move my home, and it was happening again. Our life was whisked up again, like Dorothy's in *The Wizard of Oz*, and we landed in sunbaked Tucson, Arizona, in 1967. Since we were on the other side of the country, I hoped racial strife wouldn't follow us. In Tucson a few minorities were black, but most had brown skin, and many spoke only in Spanish. I hoped this might be a place to raise our son and show him that the color of one's skin shouldn't matter. But of course there is no evading the forces of change, sometimes violent. Martin Luther King, Jr. was assassinated in Memphis, Tennessee, in 1968. Many saddened people of America were ashamed when Lester Maddox, the governor of Georgia, refused to close the state government in honor of the native Atlanta civil rights leader. He felt that MLK was "an enemy of the state" and didn't attend his funeral.

My husband's mother picked out a house for us to buy, and I flew out west with our six-week-old son. My husband packed up our things in Atlanta and drove a truck with our dog and parakeet to our new place in Tucson. I didn't have anything to do with the choice of a house but was so overwhelmed with taking care of our new son that I let everyone else take charge of the move. When my mother-in-law indicated that we were on the "good" side of town, I just nodded and wondered what the "bad" side of town must be like.

Our small, three-bedroom block house was clean but had ugly mustard-colored wall-to-wall carpeting and dingy cream-colored drapes. The front yard was covered with a few cacti and white rocks, like the neighbors'. However, the backyard had potential, since it was enclosed with a big wall suitable for our dog and growing son. We got moved in, and I recognized quickly that many of the customs and ways of life were different in this part of the country. I welcomed that.

Most of the houses in this dry, hot climate were cooled by evaporative coolers instead of air conditioners, and most had gravel front yards. Some people spray painted the rocks green to resemble the grass that they didn't have to mow. I learned you had to shake your shoes out each morning to make sure scorpions weren't nesting there and to be careful not to pick any flowers off cactus unless you had leather gloves on.

We found the best Mexican restaurants, where dancers twirled their colorful costumes to the music of the strolling mariachis. These musicians sang and played guitars while we ate burritos, chimichangas, and empenadas. I enjoyed every selection on the menus, but I could never bring myself to eat the traditional menudo soup that was made from beef tripe (cows' stomachs) that some say is a good cure from a hangover.

My family and I loved the local customs and traditions of the Southwest. Easter in Tucson begins its celebration at sunrise on Good Friday with the annual procession up Sentinel Peak. People dressed in costumes from the time of Christ follow a man carrying a cross to the top of the mountain. This walk is a re-enactment of Jesus going to his place of crucifixion. The cross stays at the top until Easter morning, when people climb the mountain for a sunrise service.

One Mexican Christmas tradition is the celebration of Las Posadas. A child is dressed as an angel and leads children, depicted as Mary and Joseph, though the historic barrio looking for a place to spend the night. They go door to door and finally find a place and reenact the story of Christmas. Cinco de Mayo is another popular celebration throughout Mexico. In Tucson it is a festival of American-Mexican heritage. The Day of the Dead is celebrated about the same time as Halloween and gives people time to remember and honor deceased relatives. Parades and special foods are part of both of these ceremonies.

I learned if you were Mexican in Tucson you were not welcome in some organizations or social circles. The majority of Mexicans lived on the south and southwest side of town. Schools were integrated, but if you were the only Mexican in the classroom, some teachers could look down or even ignore you. Most of the Mexican children attended schools that were on "their" side of town, much like the blacks did in the schools in the South. I told myself it seemed like racism was alive even in this part of the country, only with a different hue of brown. I still could not answer this question for myself: Is distrust and prejudice taught by a culture, or is it part of our animal human nature?

We visited the Papago Indian tribe, west of the city, and joined them in their saguaro fruit gathering season. The Indians took tents, cooking supplies, and tools that they used for picking and cooking the fruit of the giant "signature" cactus of southern Arizona and camped for a few weeks in the saguaro forest. We drove out early and joined them around their campfire. The coffee they offered us was strong, but the freshly baked empanadas melted in your mouth. Soon an old woman dressed in a cotton skirt and colorful blouse came out of the tent. Her black hair was covered with a scarf that was tied under her dark brown chin. Someone whispered to me, "She's 95 years old and still comes out here every year."

The old lady found her way to what I thought was a pile of sticks and picked up a ten-foot-long wooden pole. That seemed to be the signal it was time to go and pick the red juicy fruit from the top of the tall saguaros. They used the long poles to snap the fruit right off the tall cactus arms. These red bulbs were taken back to the fire and roasted on a metal pan or put into a pot of liquid and stirred until it became a thick jelly. We left in late afternoon with a jar of homemade saguaro jelly and a thankful heart that we were able to experience this tradition, which was unfortunately dying at that time.

Life in the desert can be trying. Water is the most important resource many of the Indians have. During one of the severe droughts while we were there, the cattle were left stranded without food or water. The people didn't have the resources to take hay and water out to the dying animals and called for volunteers to assist them. We loaded our truck with hay, stopped by the Indian Affairs office, and picked up barrels of water. The rutted road led far out into the mesquite trees to the dehydrated and starving cattle. We filled the water troughs, left the hay, then went back to the office and picked up more water and hay. I'm not sure this effort made much difference, but somehow we felt a connected to these Indians and their struggle to make a place for themselves in this world.

We also spent many hours on the beaches in Mexico. The first time we drove there was on an Easter Sunday, the day of one of the biggest celebrations in Mexico. The border city of Nogales was only sixty miles from Tucson and was filled with residents and Americans. The streets were guarded on each corner by Mexican police, with automatic long guns. They stopped every car and van to check for weapons and drugs. When the guard pulled our motor home over and stepped inside, I nervously opened a map some-one had given us and pointed to the beach where most Americans stayed. I didn't speak much Spanish, but the guard, in broken English, told us how to get to the designated gringo beach. After a quick search of our RV, he left. We hoped he was telling us the truth and drove off in the direction that he told us.

The beach was beautiful, with cream-colored sand that went on for miles and miles without one structure in sight. The tide was so extreme that when it was low you could walk for a mile toward the ocean until you reached water. There you could collect shells and see all kinds of stranded sea critters struggling to get to the water. During the day, Mexicans came selling trinkets, blankets, and shrimp. At night, Butch and Billy and I sat by a bonfire to watch the iridescent glow of microscopic organisms that the waves brought in. We were one with nature and far away from any.

The Seri Indians of Sonora, Mexico, are remarkable; they survive in the harshest conditions. They live in the dry, hot desert and have tried to keep most of their traditions alive. People told us about the plight of these peo-ple and their need for food and clothing, so we collected canned goods, jugs of water, and clothes, then headed down into the back country. We passed mesquite trees, organ pipe cactus, large saguaro cactus, and iron-wood trees that lived to be hundreds of years old. As we turned down a side road, we saw several tar-paper shacks in the distance and a few people sitting under porches with mesquite branches that covered the roofs. The ocean wasn't too far away, and we could smell the salty air.

Women in long skirts and thin blouses ran to us holding up necklaces and trinkets, wanting us to buy something. Our son climbed in the back of the truck and began handing out clothes and food. Some young boys came and took jugs of water to their shacks. We purchased some ironwood carv-ings and baskets from them, knowing this money would buy some extra food for the next few days.

I had lived in the South and had seen a lot of poverty in the black com-munities, of course, but the poverty of these dark-skinned Indians was the most intense I'd ever seen. Even so, they chose to stay and continue their traditions in this community. I knew that as the older people died, the younger ones would probably move out into a more convenient world, but one that would be more complicated than this one.

I was a stay-at-home mother until our son was in middle school, then I got a job in the inner city teaching fourth grade. There were a few families who lived in small houses in this part of town, but many lived in government-assisted projects or old duplexes and apartments. The population of this area consisted of low-income families, single mothers, disabled parents, known felons, and families on government subsidies.

My classroom was a mixture of learning abilities and backgrounds. There were Vietnamese, Mexicans, blacks, and white children. One of the white children was the son of a member of the notorious Hells Angels bike organization. His father wore the typical uniform: leather jacket, leather pants, and kerchief tied around his head. He dropped his son off at school each morning, then sped away in a great diesel bike roar. Both the mother and father attended every event their son was in and even brought cookies to the class on special days. One white girl's mothers were lesbians and were very protective about their tiny girl, who wore thick horn-rimmed glasses. One tall boy's parents couldn't read, and they would come to me after school and have me read to them.

A very small black boy who missed a lot of school would always stir up problems. He seemed very angry and would get in fights at recess. Once he came to me and said that another boy grabbed his arm and hit him. He said, "Look at my arm where he got me. It's turning black." I looked at his arm and rubbed it, but I couldn't see any black bruise on his black arm.

The children complained about him and said that he kept sticking them with something. I didn't see anything, but each time I walked by him in the aisle, I felt a sharp stick on my leg. Then I saw he had put straight pins in the tips of his shoes so he could stick the person passing by. Not very happily, I asked him, "How did you learn to do that?" He told me, "My older brother puts knives on the ends of his shoes and could really get you."

This was the time when the "boat children" from Vietnam were brought to the United States. These families were fleeing the Vietcong invasion and turmoil. A Christian organization in Tucson sponsored families from Vietnam and made provision for some to be placed in our school. I had two students whose families fled the country in boats as bombs exploded around them. These children spoke no English and were traumatized from their experiences. One of my students lost his hearing because of the noise of the shells falling around him as he crouched down in the bottom of the boat that was carrying him and his family to safety.

The school district had an interpreter, Mrs. Hooker, who came to the school once a week and helped the students with their lessons. The Vietnamese children loved her and would rush to her when she showed up on the playground. Mrs. Hooker told me that some of the older English-speaking children taught the immigrants profane and unacceptable words. This interpreter said, "One day the children came running from the playground when they saw me. They shouted, 'Here comes the bitch! Here comes the bitch!'" She laughed and continued, "They thought this was a loving term."

Since I had taught music before, I was assigned the school's Christmas and spring programs. The cafeteria was always filled with parents and relatives who came early to get a good seat. But some parents couldn't or wouldn't come to the performance, and their children would have a difficult time getting transportation to the school. I told the choir members, "If you can get here for the performance, I will make sure you have a ride back home. I don't want you walking home in the dark."

There were always a few whom I had to drive home. One ten-year-old African American boy was one of these. He lived in a three-story red brick building in a government project. His father was in jail, and his mother had to stay home with the other children. The program was over about 9 o'clock, and I loaded the car with several children. I dropped all of them off then drove to the project where Sherard lived. I pulled into the parking lot, got out of the car, and began walking to the sidewalk. He rushed up to me and said, "Mrs. Watts, I can go the rest of the way by myself. You just go on back to the car."

I looked down at him and said, "Sherard, I can't let you go there by yourself."

He lived in one of two long brick buildings that were parallel to each other with a narrow walk separating them. Small windows, that probably never got any direct sun, looked over the walkway. The buildings had different sections where steps led to concrete stoops. Large white numbers plastered the gray metal doors that opened to dark stairs and apartments.

There weren't any lights along the sidewalk, and I became nervous. Sherard held my hand and said, "Mrs. Watts, see that window up there with the light on." He pointed to the third floor, then continued, "If he starts shooting, run to one of the stoops and hide next to it."

Sherard stopped at one of the buildings and said, "This is where I live." He walked up the steps and went inside. As soon as the metal door closed, I ran back to my car and skidded out of the parking lot. The memory of this small fourth-grade African American boy trying to protect his school-teacher will stay with me forever.

It was the end of the school year when the seventh- and eighth-grade middle school had an open house for the following year's new students. The sixth-grade choir at my elementary school was invited to sing for the parents at the assembly. We had practiced the songs, and I reminded them to wear a nice shirt that didn't have any typical sayings, symbols, or words on the front. I asked the choir to meet at the middle school thirty minutes before the performance, and someone would tell them which room to go to.

The principal of the school directed the students to the chemistry room. There I was, with forty-five hyperactive children, in a room with glass tubes, assorted liquids, and strange-looking displays waiting thirty minutes for our entry on stage. Surprisingly, no chemicals were spilled and no bottles of preserved specimens were destroyed. I lined the children up and was getting ready to escort them to the cafeteria for the assembly when Henry, a tall African American boy, climbed inside through a back window. He came to me and said, "I'm sorry I'm late. My uncle just got out of prison and we had a party for him." I looked at him and said, "Henry, how did you get in the schoolyard with all of the scissor wire around the building?"

"Mrs. Watts," he proceeded to tell me, "it's no problem if you know what to do."

Henry had a white t-shirt that was ripped and covered with grass, dirt, and little splotches of blood. I didn't care that his shirt was not "nice." He was there!

At that time, Tucson had several gangs, but the main ones were the Bloods and the Crips. The Bloods, with red shirts and bandanas, consisted mainly of blacks and Mexicans. The Crips were usually whites; their attire was blue. Most of the gang activity was on the west and southwest side of town, so my family stayed away from that area.

Later, I began teaching music in a middle school that bordered the southwest side of town. The school had some African Americans and many Hispanics, and the rest were whites. The music room also served as a center for general music as well as for choir rehearsals. When I entered the room on my first day, I scanned the room and saw the red and blue chairs that were stacked against the wall. I carefully pulled the chairs down and arranged them in rows, then moved my desk to a corner of the room. After a few more adjustments, everything seemed to be ready for classes.

When the bell rang on the first day, the students rushed in and began pushing chairs around. One Hispanic student shouted, "I'm not sitting in that Crip chair!" as he pointed to a blue chair. One white student pointed to a red chair and said, "I'm not sitting on that Blood chair." I finally realized the influence gangs had on these twelve-year-old students. We had a discussion and decided that the students had to sit in alphabetical order but could choose the color of chair they wanted.

I always taught the musical *West Side Story* to my eighth graders. We studied the music and lyrics and compared the musical to Shakespeare's *Romeo and Juliet*, then viewed the movie. I passed out lyrics to the songs so they could follow the singing, and I sat back to watch. As soon as the first gang fight came on in the movie, papers and pencils started flying across the room, and students started shouting at each other. This was a "war" of the Latino gang and the white gang that was being replayed in my classroom. Again, I had to intervene, and we discussed the underlying meaning of *West Side Story* and then compared it to *Romeo and Juliet*. Now I was prepared for the students' reactions to anything race or gang related.

The school district invited my eighth-grade choir to sing for its executive luncheon. There were four eighth-grade boys in the choir who liked to sing together and rehearsed as a group in one of their parents' garages. The buses couldn't take the entire choir, so I asked the boys if they would perform. We loaded the mics and other musical equipment into my van and set it up at the hotel meeting room. The boys performed their song with their hip-hop dance routine and were met with great applause.

While the applause continued, I said to them, "Go on up and introduce yourselves."

They asked, "What do we say?" I said, "Just tell them your names." The boys walked up and stood in front of the mic, and one said, "We are the BMWs." I panicked. Was this a gang name? I had never heard them use that name.

But he continued, "We are Black, Mexican, and White, and we all get along together."

The audience became unglued and stood with a thunderous applause.

Even here, away from the segregated South, skin color seemed to interfere with life. But maybe this incident was a sign that all hope for racial cooperation was not lost. Maybe, little by little, the chain will be broken, and the next generation will be more tolerant of differences and "We all get along together" will be a byword.

Erv on AM Catnip in 1982. He was building high-end homes in this desert country, but what he loved to do was ride at a friend's riding center.

All around us was beauty in this southwestern state. Out our window were the Catalina Mountains.

I took an environmental class at the University of Arizona in 1987. We traveled to Mexico as part of the class. Here a local musician is playing the accordion in the village of Punta de la Libertad in Mexico.

I loved working with chorus groups. This one is the 6th grade at John B. Wright School in Tucson. We sang at concerts and visited malls.

A woman our family watched, boiling suguaro cactus juice to make jelly in 1990. Many shades of brown were in Arizona's faces, and I loved them all. She is a member of the Tohono O'odham nation, formerly called (by the white man)
Papagos.

BMW group performing at Secrist Middle School in the 1990s. I was afraid BMW might mean they were a gang, but their initials meant Black, Mexican and White.

Bill on AM Able Seaman. He is in his mid-thirties in this photo. We left Arizona in 2003, traveling in a motor home to see America and enjoyed the vagabond life.

BACK TO INDIANA

Butch and I had lived in Tucson for thirty-five years when we decided it was time to downsize. I retired from teaching, my husband closed his business, and then we sold the house. Our son Bill was grown and living in Franklin, Indiana, not too far south of Indianapolis. We purchased a thirty-four-foot motor home, then, nervously, began to wonder where we were going. As I began packing the RV, I remembered Woody Guthrie's folk song, "This Land Is Your Land" and began singing, "From the redwood forest to the gulf stream waters. This land was made for you and me." Then I knew we were going to be vagabonds and experience the country. We took one last look at the house as we drove down the driveway, then started down "that ribbon of highway" with our two cats and their litter box.

We toured the west coast, the northwest, the Dakotas, the Midwest, and national monuments and parks. When we parked at night in campgrounds, we got to talk with many people who shared their hopes, experiences, and plans for their future. After six months, our wanderlust began to wane. Our only granddaughter was now two months old, and heartstrings began drawing the motor home to a stop. We were headed to Indiana, back where we started our married life forty years ago. This time we would settle in Franklin.

The one-hundred-year-old farmhouse we bought was in the middle of fourteen acres of corn fields and only a ten-minute drive to our son's house. I had lived in the country as a child and in the desert countryside in Tucson, but I had never lived in the middle of a cornfield. I told my husband, "You know what teachers say, 'Just another learning experience.'" We got settled, and I began to wonder about the customs and traditions of this midwestern part of the country. Had things changed since we had lived here years ago? Had people's attitudes changed? I was determined to find out.

There was so much to learn about this community and so many places to explore. People were very friendly and offered advice such as the best way to kill crabgrass or the best tomato plants to buy. But we were surprised at one of the first questions they asked: "Which church do you go to?" The first question people asked when we lived in Tucson was, "Where are you from?" I think this was because so many people there were newcomers. It seemed like there was a church on every block in this Indiana community. The Saturday paper even designated a whole page to the directions and times of Sunday services for all the churches nearby. I did notice that there was one African Methodist Episcopal Church in the neighborhood and wondered how many people of color attended it.

One day we were at a restaurant and began talking to a couple seated at a table next to us. The lady was a friendly but chatty person and told me about her Homemakers Club. I had never even heard about Homemakers and wondered if this was a new type of organization in the Midwest. She then proceeded to invite me to one of its meetings at a member's shelter house for a pitch-in. I didn't know anyone, so I thought this might be a good way to meet some people.

There were so many questions I had about this organization and its shelter house. What kind of shelter was this? What were they going to do at this meeting? What was I supposed to take to the meeting? In Tucson I had assisted at abused women's shelters and pet shelters. I pitched in and cleaned the shelters and helped with distributing food and clothing for the women. Maybe this member's shelter house was like one of those.

The morning of the meeting, I pulled on a pair of work jeans and old sweatshirt that said, "We Help," then loaded my little blue truck with buckets and rags. I followed the directions the lady gave me, then turned off the paved country road onto a muddy path. Cars were parked in the wet grass next to an unpainted wooden building with windows propped open with long poles. I thought, "Surely, this must be a pet shelter. No people should be living here."

I got out of my truck and made my way to the door, where my new friend greeted me. Then I realized these rustic buildings called shelter houses were used by owners for picnics and get-togethers like this one. Inside was a group of twenty women in "Saturday-go-to-town" outfits. A mountain of food was stacked on a side table with little signs printed with the name of each dish. I made my way down the row of chairs as twenty sets of eyes followed me and sat down between two elderly women who had walkers folded next to them.

The president of the group began the meeting with a lesson, "How to make pie crusts." I sat amazed and whispered to myself, "I've never made a pie crust in my whole life." One of the elderly ladies next to me pointed and shouted, "She said she's never made a pie crust in her life." Again, these same twenty sets of eyes stared at me. The elderly lady on the other side of me turned and patted me on the knee. "Don't worry, honey. You can buy them in the grocery store, and they are just as good."

I had hoped this would be a good community for our granddaughter to grow up in. Yes, I found some of the same intolerant attitudes I've come to recognize in many people as I grew up and traveled, including myself. Yet this town had family values, a low crime rate, and access to cultural events, and I found activities like community choir and the county museum, in which I could do satisfying volunteer work. There are good people everywhere, and I found them in Franklin, too.

We moved here so we would be a part of our granddaughter's everyday life and add to her memories. When Addie was born, I told her parents that I wanted to be called Grammy...she was my "Grammy Award." At first, when she began to talk she said "Amm," then "Ammy," and finally, it became "Mammy." Every time she calls me by my name, Mammy, I smile and think about all of those black southern mammies who took care of white babies and loved them as if they were their own. Then I think about all of those white children who loved their black mammies and nestled into their bosoms while they were rocked to sleep. No matter who you are, when you hear the word Mammy you think of comforting love.

Whenever Addie was at our house, we would play dress up, have tea parties, ride the horses, and play in the mud. I knew these were the formative years for children, and my husband and I wanted her to grow up with ethical learning. Her parents had already begun teaching her right from wrong and how to love one another. At every opportunity, I would sneak in examples of what it means to be tolerant of others' feelings. One day when she was in second grade, I picked her up after school and talked about Martin Luther King and the civil rights movement. She sat quietly for a few minutes, then said, "You know Jackie, one of my friends in class? She's black, and if it wasn't for Martin Luther King, she wouldn't be able to be in my school." It was then that I felt she understood the plight of these minorities, even if it was only in a second-grade mentality.

Now she is in high school. I have never been more proud of her than when she told me that the group of students she eats lunch with calls themselves the International group. "Our group is from China, Mexico, India, the United States," she chuckled and continued, "and one who is a Cajun from South Louisiana." This brought back memories of the four boys in my middle school choir who told an audience, "We are the BMWs... Black, Mexican, and White, and we all get along."

One afternoon we settled down on the sofa and I pulled out the DVD of *South Pacific*. Rogers and Hammerstein's musical opened on Broadway in 1949 and received a Pulitzer Prize the next year for best drama. Some people boycotted the play because it dealt with racial issues and interracial marriages. One of the songs is titled, "You've Got To Be Carefully Taught."

You've got to be carefully taught
To hate and fear, you've got to be taught from year to year.
It's got to be drummed in your little ear...
You've got to be taught to be afraid of people
Whose eyes are oddly made
And whose skin is a different shade...

Someone said that every child doesn't want to become president, but every child should have the opportunity to become what he wants to be. I am confident the new generation will be given the opportunity to grow up and see the possibility of equality. People say children are born colorblind. I think they see all of the colors. When these little ones look at a garden of flowers, they see all the different hues and love them all. Martin Luther King taught that some day we will be able to see people not as black people and white people but as human beings. Children are the same except for the skin color.

WHAT COLOR IS GOD'S SKIN by Wilkers and Stevenson
Good Night I said to my little son
So tired out when the day was done
Then he said, as I tucked him in

Tell me, Mommy...What Color is God's Skin?
CHORUS
What color is God's skin?
What color is God's skin?
I said it's black, brown, it's yellow...it's red, it is white
Every man's the same in the good Lord's sight.
He looked at me with those shining eyes
I knew that I could tell no lies
He said Mommy tell me why the different races fight
If we're the same in the good Lord's sight?
CHORUS
"Son, he said, that is part of our suffering past
But the whole human family is learning at last
That the thing we missed on the road we trod
Was to walk as the daughters and the sons of God

As I look at my life's long journey, I hear echoes of voices of famous people: "I have a dream." "Ask what you can do for your country." "All tyranny needs to gain a foothold is for people of good conscience to remain silent." "Be not afraid." "The only fear we have to fear is fear is itself." "It's hard to fail, but it is worse never to have tried to succeed." "Love your neighbor as yourself."

Then I hear voices from my own past: "If you hit her, then you will have to hit me." "I'll move to the front of the bus." "Would you sign my autograph book?" "We are the BMWs, and we all get along." "Mammy." "Honey, I wasn't alone. My Lord was with me."

Listening to these echoes, I see that we all peer at life through different kinds of prisms. Some people are optimistic and only see good reflections, but some complain that the reflections are tainted or miscued. They think the beds they see in these broken images would be more comfortable if they would buy designer comforters and cover the old feather mattress. If only they would realize that no matter how they cover it up, it will always remain a lumpy feather mattress on an old antique bed frame from days past.

I feel hope when I think about the black, brown, and white young people who marched shoulder to shoulder, showing the world they all can work together regardless of the color of their skin. Black hands were clasping white hands; white arms were entwined with brown ones; brown faces were pressed against tear-stained ones. They all might have looked at the world through different glasses but knew that everyone wanted the same things, a little quilted patch of happiness. Maybe it is through them and the different lenses they put on that will help all of us focus on justice and equality.

We all can hope, pray, and work toward that vision.

When Bill married Kathy, they moved to Franklin, Indiana, in the 1990s. Eventually we wanted to be with him and his wife and our granddaughter Addie. Here she is shown with her dog Mocha at Myrtle Beach.
I've tried to share with her some of the values I had to learn the hard way.